LETTERS TO HIS DAUGHTER

By luck, intelligence or intuition, my brothers and I always recognised in our father a man of whom to be proud, and a man whose opinion was of great value. It was often hard to maintain good relations, but it was always important to us to do so and to evoke his admiration—because admiration from someone like my father, in whose judgement we put great faith, gave us great satisfaction and happiness. And because he never failed to believe in us and love us, it was as important to him that he retain our trust and friendship.

This also had its problems. My father set high standards for himself and for us. He was a perfectionist in all he did and he required the same perfection from us. When our inertia led us into poor grades at school, or our laziness left a project half-finished or we scamped a job that we had been given, we knew that we had failed him and he made it clear that he felt the same. So our displeasure at ourselves for doing badly became directed into resentment against our father for requiring high standards and demanding so much from us. Again we would clash and quarrel. Life would have been so much easier for us, and so much less satisfying and rewarding, had he taken less interest in our lives and asked less of us.

**Also by the same author,
and available in Coronet Books:**

In the Country

Letters to his Daughter

Kenneth Allsop

CORONET BOOKS
Hodder and Stoughton

Copyright © 1974 by the Estate of Kenneth Allsop
Compilation and Introduction © 1974 by Amanda Allsop

First published by Hamish Hamilton 1974

Coronet edition 1975

This book is sold subject to the condition that it shall not, by way of trade or otherwise, be lent, re-sold, hired out or otherwise circulated without the publisher's prior consent in any form of binding or cover other than that in which this is published and without a similar condition including this condition being imposed on the subsequent purchaser.

Printed and bound in Great Britain for
Coronet Books, Hodder and Stoughton,
St. Paul's House, Warwick Lane,
London, EC4P 4AH
By Richard Clay (The Chaucer Press), Ltd.,
Bungay, Suffolk

ISBN 0 340 19921 0

DEDICATION

Although this is my father's book—he wrote it—I would like to take the liberty of assuming role of authorship and dedicating it to him, and to my mother.

Introduction

WHEN my brothers and I were young children, we scarcely knew our father. At the end of 1950—when we were all less than four years old—he joined the now sadly defunct 'Picture Post', and the work he was doing there took him away from home—frequently abroad—for long periods of time. So inevitably he figured in our lives only as a remote and rarely-present stranger, but who was, nevertheless, formidable in confrontation and in spirit when he was absent; and who, we knew well, held final veto and absolute power in the family. I can clearly remember his arrivals home, and the excitement and pleasure they evoked. His physical presence at home, though, is a dim shadow—and I suppose I thought that he wasn't much more aware of us than we were of him. I was therefore astonished when I recently discovered a great number of letters he had written to our doctors, teachers, headmasters, tutors. It had never before occurred to me that he took such an active interest in our lives, because we, in our early years, never received tangible proof of his interest.

He always sent us brief postcards from whichever part of the world he happened to be visiting; and he never failed to bring us presents home. We, in our turn, wrote to him—presumably because we really did miss him. We were conscious that we didn't have a father around very often, and that this was not normal among our friends (and also that life was more interesting when he was around). However, as we barely knew him, we didn't especially miss him as a person.

Our lack of contact with him eliminated any orthodox father/child relationship. But we were always very aware of the strength and dominance of his personality, and equally conscious of his violent temper—though only once did he ever hit any of us. I must confess that he was perfectly justified on that occasion; my younger brother and I were fighting, tearing each other apart, on the kitchen floor, and causing an obstruction, and the only way my father could separate us was to grab each of us and wrench us apart.

My father's frequent absences were not the cause of our difficulties in knowing him as a parent—or his difficulties in knowing us as children. They merely heightened already-existent factors. He was an only child, brought up by a Yorkshire mother who, though loving him dearly, despised any display of affection and was therefore unable to give to him the open warmth that every child needs, and would certainly have insisted upon similar restraint of feeling from him. Added to that was his inwardly-directed—perhaps self-absorbed—mind, and the two working together caused his basic difficulties in communicating, especially with small children, who obviously hadn't learnt to converse intellectually, nor to follow accepted codes and rules of superficial social conversation. He couldn't relate to the irrational mechanic of children's minds, and was always scared of them and uncomfortable with them. The loss of his leg, too, was a barrier to relationship, in that he was physically unable to romp with us or to kick a ball about.

This is not to suggest that he didn't love us—he did, very much. His concern and care for us emerged in other ways, less direct—in those letters to our teachers, his presents, his cards to us. And we showed our love for him in similar ways—in our letters to him; in our delight when he did return; in our constant desire to please him, engendered not only by fear, which was sometimes the case, but also because we somehow knew that he was a remarkable man, and that his love and respect were worth earning.

He wanted his family; and when he did take time off to spend with us, he did it wholeheartedly. He was never enthralled by dolls and train-sets, and he never attempted or pretended to be. But he took a great delight in introducing us to his interests. From my earliest memories I have pictures in my mind of sitting in front of the record player listening to Louis Armstrong and Billie Holliday, my father explaining and interpreting them with his usual passion and earnestness, determined that we should love what he loved. His way of expressing his love for us was to share with us his own pleasures. We were not always as receptive as we might have been. I remember, when I was older, an exceedingly tedious and uncomfortable evening of John Coltrane, from whom, I'm afraid, I did not derive the same pleasure as my father.

His anxiety that we should all thoroughly and completely enjoy family events (as dictated by him) did at times become a terrific ordeal and burden to us all. If any one of us showed signs of boredom or disinterest, he was acutely disconcerted, and he let us know it. He made us feel that it was a failing in ourselves and perhaps felt it a failing in himself. He found it hard to acknowledge difference of interest or of mood. But generally, his incisiveness and vigour, once he had entered upon a particular activity, was highly infectious. We caught his mood of enthusiasm and involvement.

Life when he was around became a series of 'special occasions' put into operation with great care to detail, and each occasion was enacted to the perfection my father always required. A country walk became a mammoth expedition. We would set out, each laden with wellingtons, heavy coats, binoculars, cameras, birdbooks, on a five-hour trek across mudtracks, through brambles and bushes into forests to discover a hawk pellet, a buzzard's nest or a badger sett—to general rejoicing at the discovery of any sign of wildlife. (Though, sadly for Kenneth, and now to my own regret, none of us could fully share his great passion for birds. My younger brother showed more interest than the rest of us, but he never followed it with the same dedication as his father.)

Christmas was the most important ritual of all, and for all of us the most exciting. It was the one day in the year, every year, that was assuredly ours; that the family was certain to be together. For no matter what assignments were required of him, he always made sure that he was home on Christmas day; and together we lived out his dream of a Dickensian Christmas, with heavily-decked rooms of paper chains and holly; stocking presents, and then the parcels under the Christmas tree, branches over-adorned with tinsel and silver balls, my father presiding and handing out presents. Nuts, sweets, chocolates, dates and a huge dinner, again presided over by my father, the table strewn with streamers, the remnants of crackers, paper hats; and games and music. And somehow, however dismal life was at the time and however badly my father's work was going, we all managed to feel festive-spirited.

The fear of mishap did, as I have said, create tension. In so many ways Kenneth was a Victorian at heart. He developed an image of his family and his role in that family very much in the Victorian spirit, and it was often difficult to play one's part to his satisfaction, though it continued to be important to us that we should live up to his expectations. Unfortunately, ideals are never actualised, and we weren't—and never could have been—the ideal children he had created in his mind. None the less, I don't think he would have been happy with those dream-children. He wanted us to be different and special, but only according to his pattern. We were to be individuals, and he strongly encouraged this, but then found it hard to accept that our individuality implied that we could not adhere to his mould. Concurrent with his confusion between disappointment at our non-conformity to his pattern, and probable reluctant gladness that we had our own minds and wills, we, in our turn, fluctuated between fear of his disappointment and resentment that we should have to work so hard and conscientiously at pleasing him. Under our mother's upbringing, we were given freedom based on what she knew of our different personalities; under our father's, our awareness of the freedom we had was tempered by the knowledge that we had to control our instincts and consequent behaviour according to a strict pattern. Consequently our relationship with him was one of great emotional and mental confusion. None of us knew exactly where we stood with him—or he with us.

As we grew older, and reached our teens, our attitude to him—and his to us—changed. He did not cease to be a perfectionist or an idealist as a father, but we did begin to get to know and understand each other. He was more frequently at home, and so we grew more familiar with him and became used to having him around. In earlier years he had felt very keenly an exclusion from the family—not unnaturally; his frequent absences cut him off from day-to-day family activities. Around the beginning of the 1960s he became very conscious that he had missed out on what he had come to realise was the core of his life, and he began to work hard at becoming part of the family. It is difficult to make the transition from the position of comparative stranger, on somewhat formal terms, to that of a close relation and friend. The transition was the harder for him because he had never found close friendships easy to make or maintain. He had an abundance of acquaintances but very few intimate companions. It was therefore hard for all of us to make such a drastic change in our relationship. We never fully achieved a state of easy expression of affection and trust —though we did all learn to believe that the affection and trust existed. Though he still failed to play the Father Figure—and we failed to be his ideal children—

we grew much closer. He found it easier to talk to us as we became near-adults than when we were children. He enjoyed intellectual conversation with us—on books, politics, music, art—and we enjoyed his conversation and found it stimulating and exciting. He became very interested in our school work, too, giving encouragement when we needed it and stern lectures when he thought we were slacking. Because of his overt and genuine interest we were always glad to talk to him about it. We would read the typescripts of his articles and the proofs of his books and comment on them, and he always took notice of our comments—and began, when we diverted our interests into particular channels, to come to us for advice on our 'special' subjects. He took an interest in what we thought and what we did, distinct from what he thought we should do and think. We became a part of each other's lives as individuals in our own right and less as part of an image.

He still wielded ultimate authority, which became more directly wielded than it was during our childhood. He was totally intolerant of laziness, and of time-wasting. He would fly into a rage if he found us watching television on a sunny afternoon—or, for that matter, at any time. Because of his conviction that we were all highly intelligent and talented in our different ways, he was ruthless on mental effort and discipline in work. He would be sincerely distressed when he thought that we were not fully using our innate abilities to the full, not experiencing life to the full—and especially when he thought that we were not expressing ourselves clearly and with proper respect for the English language, in which he delighted. He was forever correcting our speech and grammar. He himself loved words, treated them adoringly and used them carefully. Good grammar and well-constructed speech were important to him not for their own sake, nor as a sign of good breeding, but because they symbolised to him well-developed and well-constructed thought. If we spoke carelessly or imprecisely or with disregard to pronunciation we were pulled up sharply and corrected. Expression of thought became his profession because it was so important to him, and it agonised him to hear us mistreating language, using sloppy slang and enunciating badly. We were badgered constantly and became terribly conscious in his presence of each sentence we uttered; which tended to discourage us from uttering sentences at all, so his aim was often unintentionally self-defeating.

He bullied and bludgeoned us all the time, not over social standards of behaviour (although many of his Victorian dreams extended into adulthood, and he would have loved us to be adept in social graces, these were not of principal importance). He bullied over what was of interest to him and what he believed would interest and assist us. I remember, when I was about thirteen years old, driving with him unwillingly into Stevenage to search the record shops for a newly-released single by a then unknown pop group called the Beatles, which he insisted I should hear. So often he picked up on fads and innovations long before we did—and long before they became popular.

Because I tended to gabble unintelligibly, he decided that I should take elocution lessons to improve my speech. I did so, again reluctantly at his insistence, and then became totally and fervently immersed in drama and the theatre. Later on when my father was becoming worried about my lack of confidence and resultant withdrawal into myself, he came home with literature on the National Youth Theatre, having already resolved that I should join, and nagged me into applying for an audition with them. Eventually, after his continual persuasive nagging, I did apply, and was accepted by them, and have been grateful ever since to him. The seasons I spent with the National Youth Theatre were some of the happiest and fullest periods of my life.

It took all of us a long time to realise that his pushing and bullying, and intolerantly persistent pronouncements that we occupy our time and minds in a certain way or go to a particular country or read a particular book, was more often than not engendered by a sincere concern and the best intentions for us.

Despite his impatience and intolerance of carelessness and laziness, Kenneth was a constant support to us in times of crisis—major or minor. We couldn't release our adolescent emotional problems on him; there was no basis of understanding on either side; but in any practical way he could possibly help us, he did. If we had brought trouble upon ourselves we were not let off lightly with a pat on the head. But after he had lectured us long, loudly and severely, he would put all his energy into getting us out of our difficulties.

His motives in helping and supporting us so loyally were not, obviously, totally altruistic. He wanted us to have the best of opportunities, access to as much experience as possible, and the best education he could give us. Like many fathers, most of all he wanted for us those things which he felt that he himself had lacked; and for us to succeed where he felt himself to have failed. These ambitions for us were strongest in academic fields. He had been sent to minor private schools, where it was considered of greater importance to instil social mores than to impart a high degree of knowledge. He was nineteen years old when the second world war broke out. When it ended he was twenty-five, had lost a leg and gained a wife, and so eager and anxious to get moving with his career in journalism that he didn't take the opportunity of going to university. When my mother first met him he was twenty-one and complaining bitterly of having reached so great an age without yet having had a novel published!

Missing university was something he later deeply regretted, and he was determined that we should go. He placed particularly high value on university education for us, both for our own sakes—for the essential development of personality and mind he believed it would give us—and also because he needed us in a sense to represent him. Oxford and Cambridge had always symbolised to him the whole essence of intellectual brilliance and absolute social refinement, and he was very anxious that my older brother and myself should get into one of them (my younger brother was from early on leaning towards Art). Neither of us made either university, and I think he always felt some disappointment in us for failing to be the intellectual successes he had decided we should be. Perhaps his disappointment was lessened when he won a Research Fellowship to Oxford. Eventually he grew to accept that we were happy, and had found social and educational fulfilment at our respective modern universities, and he concerned himself with our time there as ardently and positively as he would have done had we achieved the academic brilliance he had hoped for. In fact his enthusiasm for anything in which we took an interest frequently extended beyond our own enthusiasm. Once I casually mentioned that I had read and enjoyed *Tender is the Night*. The following day my father handed me a file of newspaper cuttings on Fitzgerald and the author's complete works. Kenneth's ebullience would affect me, and in this case I read Fitzgerald avidly and talked about him with my father constantly—until a different author arose to divert our attention. We developed a close relationship based on these shared joys of experience, and used this method of communication for all levels of expression. We both found it difficult to make direct expressions of friendship and affection, so we made them indirectly. We knew that the most effective way to make up after an argument would be to bring up a newspaper item or a new book or record. We were fortunate in that, enjoying so much in common—the same literature, the same music, the same films and the same attitudes to life and people—we always had some ready grounds for conversation.

From very early in my life we used to clash continuously and furiously. I inherited from my father many of his worst qualities. We had the same inflammable and unreasonable temper, impatience and refusal to compromise. I can remember countless occasions on which I would storm away from the meal table refusing to speak to him ever again, and on which he would threaten to throw me out of the house and refuse in turn to speak to me. We could rarely apologise to each other, but we always had resort to roundabout methods, and would come to speak gradually, one of us tentatively bringing up a topic of conversation or suggesting a walk. We vocalised our anger more easily than we vocalised our love—but the love, and warmth and respect, existed nevertheless.

By luck, intelligence or intuition, my brothers and I always recognised in our father a man of whom to be proud, and a man whose opinion was of great value. It was often hard to maintain good relations, but it was always important to us to do so and to evoke his admiration—because admiration from someone like my father, in whose judgement we put great faith, gave us great satisfaction and happiness. And because he never failed to believe in us and love us, it was as important to him that he retain our trust and friendship.

This also had its problems. My father set high standards for himself and for us. He was a perfectionist in all he did and he required the same perfection from us. When our inertia led us into poor grades at school, or our laziness left a project half-finished or we scamped a job that we had been given, we knew that we had failed him and he made it clear that he felt the same. So our displeasure at ourselves for doing badly became directed into resentment against our father for requiring high standards and demanding so much from us Again we would clash and quarrel. Life would have been so much easier for us, and so much less satisfying and rewarding, had he taken less interest in our lives and asked less of us.

Because of the similarity of temperament, I quarrelled with my father more frequently than the rest of the family did. But our violent disagreements were an integral part of our relationship.

As I had so much of his personality, my father understood me very well, and I understood him. We shared a basic, implicit comprehension of each other's innate emotions and needs. Our fights were usually sparked off by a reaction against some trait which we disliked in ourselves and saw in the other. But without the bad patches, we could not have had such a good and close relationship. We might have got on perfectly well on a superficial level and avoided unpleasant, nerve-wrenching exchanges; but we would have missed out on the basic sensitivity to each other. Occasionally in letters we did voice our affection. Usually it was hedged, but it was there.

In letters and in face-to-face communication, my father sternly lectured me and advocated ways of living and behaving. But he was in no way puritanical, despite his Victorian streak which carried with it more of the latent Victorian hedonism than their veneer of puritanism. He loved life and took it seriously only insofar as he felt it should be enjoyed and ingested to the full. He loved living things—the countryside, wildlife, birds, and above all the hawks, of which the peregrine symbolised to him a freedom and beauty beyond the reach of man.

He also enjoyed many man-made pleasures: sleazy night clubs; loud jazz clubs; bright lights; parties; glittery people. He loved the cinema when he managed to get there (although he could never come to terms with the artificiality of the theatre, and had an embarrassing habit of falling asleep and snoring loudly during a play). He had a strong sense of humour which always tempered his seriousness. I could not have accepted his earnest implorings or demands without the humour which was as important a part of him. He used to enjoy embarrassing me in front of my flatmates at university by flooding me with kitsch postcards—and once an order form for plastic gnomes. One postcard he sent from Edinburgh, a picture of the castle, had a border of tartan and the comment: 'They have started to lay this tartan grass in front of the castle.' Another from Yugoslavia showed two little furry kittens sitting cutely in a red-and-yellow wooden trolley and read: 'Ljubljana—this is a charming old city where it is the tradition for all kittens to be pulled about in toy trucks . . .'

At home he enjoyed slapstick humour—large plastic spiders in the washbasin—as much as he enjoyed literary and word games. Whenever he went to the cinema and enjoyed the film, he adopted the personality of the main character and lived it with great—excessive—vigour for some time. After a particular John Wayne western, he bought himself a stetson and a low-slung belt with holster and pistol and drove the household to distraction with his exploding caps and low-pitched Texan voice for a week. He was in continual conflict between a desperate desire for a disciplined life and an uncontrollable impulsiveness which would, by midday, have destroyed his daily resolution to regulate his life. Part of his constant anxiety that we should discipline our lives stemmed, I think, from his constant desire to discipline his own.

The full complexity of Kenneth does not emerge in these letters. What they reveal is only one side of him—the side that shows concern and ambition for his children. Points emerge to show his personality along a great many lines. But in his letters to me he tried to crystallise our relationship, so that they cannot be comprehensive and give a fully-rounded picture. I hope that this introduction explains something of him that the letters miss. The letters are important in their own right. To me, they are valuable not only as reminders of him, but as lastingly helpful and valuable pieces of advice. They are an indication of his priorities, his philosophy and, at times, of the way in which he tried to live out his life and encouraged me to live mine. They have ceased to be private because they are of a relevance general to all who are concerned about the problems of living.

At the time of my father's death, I was living and writing in Dorset. I found it impossible to continue with my work afterwards, and yet needed to write, for his sake and mine. I began a personal *memoire*. But emotional and practical circumstances made that impossible. Talking to an old friend about my need to write and my problems in doing so, I happened to mention that Kenneth had been a prodigious—if spasmodic—letter-writer, and that I had kept many of his letters. This friend suggested that I publish the letters as they stand, a ready-made testimonial, instead of edging around his personality and my relationship with him.

On the whole the letters speak for themselves, but they cannot stand entirely alone. There are gaps in correspondence, and events which occurred during these breaks are not accounted for in the letters. References to certain people and occurrences need explanation. Some of the letters seem to contradict themselves and each other. What is missing is the person-to-person relationship. I have inserted short paragraphs between the letters to explain some of the apparent contradictions and bridge the gaps.

*

I would like to thank Dr James Hemming, for giving me the idea and suggesting ways of putting the letters together; my mother and brothers, for their support and encouragement of the book; and Mr Rodney Legg for helpful advice.

AMANDA ALLSOP

Identification of people and animals frequently mentioned

TRIS	my brother Tristan, two years older than I.
FABE	my brother Fabian, one year younger than I.
THE MALBERTS	David, my father's oldest Fleet Street friend, and his wife Jean, my mother's closest friend.
THE SOLOMONS	My mother's sister, Pat, and her husband, Nat.
TILLIE, DUFFY AND GALLIE	A matronly dachsund called Mathilda, her son, Macduff, and a beagle, Galadriel.

From 1958—the year my father started regular work on television—until 1969, we lived in a large Elizabethan farmhouse on the Hertfordshire/Bedfordshire border; the house was surrounded by farmland, though we owned very little of the land.

In 1961 my father was working on the manuscript of his book 'The Bootleggers'.

Gurneys, Holwell, Hitchin, Herts,
6 May 1961

My dear Mandy,

I'm so sorry I upset you at our midnight tea. I think the reason was that, after sweating at the book for about 8 hours, I was as tired as you were, and edgy and soreheaded. But I didn't want to 'get at' you. Please accept my apology—and also (what I want to mention and didn't because of feeling to have ground to a halt) my thanks for all the work in the garden today, and for helping Tris to get the mower operating today.

I hope you feel revived and refilled with energy tomorrow. Your always loving (but too often rude and irritable)
    Daddy

One year, when my father was returning from one of his working trips, he had met a Californian couple at Copenhagen airport. They talked; it emerged that they had three children corresponding in age and sex to my brothers and myself. We began to exchange letters, and, later to exchange ourselves in person. It was my turn in 1962 to visit California.

At the same time, my parents were invited to the Jamaican Independence celebrations.

We still have the painting my father mentions, which became one of his favourites.

Gurneys,
25 July 1962

Darling Poodle,

It's pouring with rain here, and I'm very resentful of you disporting yourself on Californian swimming pools—quite unfair. A heat wave was announced about two days ago. It lasted about three hours by my count, and then returned to the customary dingy grey skies, including one day of gale during which most of the apples were whipped off the tree.

Mummy and I stood on the viewing area jutting out from the airport and watched your aircraft taxi-ing down to the runway and then taking off, and then watched you zooming off Westward. I don't suppose you could have seen us, because I think you were on the right hand side of the plane, opposite to where we were. Mummy was very low-spirited about you going off, and I was too, because it's a very long way to go, however old you are. So we were delighted to have your letter and to hear that the flight went quite happily, and that you arrived safely.

Now, what's happening this end? I saw old Clarkey [the local farmer] in the lane this morning, looking very ill, poor old chap, and he has a cataract developing on his eye, and is very troubled with rheumaticks. He told me that he is intending to sell up the farm, and it's already in the hands of the agents. So now Mummy has got in touch and we're going to see if it's possible to buy some of his land. Unfortunately, the farmer who owns all those plum orchards across the valley is after it, so we don't know if we'll be able to pull it off. What I'd like to get is the field adjoining the house and including all the farm buildings, and also the strip of orchard opposite the main gates. If we could buy the whole farm (about 100 acres) we could sell off the rest, but of course it's a question of whether we could manage this financially, as the total sum might be about £10,000. Clarkey asked Mummy if we'd like to buy the ponies. I know you'd love that, wouldn't you? He wants about £100 for one of them, so I don't really know—and of course it would depend largely on whether we got the meadow to keep it, or them in. But anyway, I'll bear it in mind.

I still don't know for sure whether or not I'm going to Jamaica—all manner of confusion about the arrangements at the Kingston end, but if I do it'll probably be the middle of next week. If I get there, I'll drop you a card from somewhere it's even hotter than where you are!

The other evening we met the Malberts at a little village called Melbourn near Cambridge and had dinner with them at a rather pleasant cottage place. Last night Mummy and I went to a party given by Vere Harmsworth (Lord Rothermere's son) in Chelsea, which was quite a gay affair. Then we went and had dinner at The Village, a club in Chelsea, and I, being somewhat softened up by whisky and wine, bought a painting for 75 gns by a man called William Redgrave—a large portrait of a girl; very attractive, but I somewhat regretted it later financially speaking. Moral: always look at paintings when you're stone sober.

Do hope you're having a lovely time. We miss you very much, and the house is considerably quieter, but not better for that. We gather that Pam is now there, so that'll be more fun for you, having a girl of your own age to be with. I wonder how you're reacting to America—it's a very strange and stupendous experience, as I remember my first time there. Do try to keep up a diary of your impressions and reactions and experiences. You'll find it terrifically interesting to look back later at it; and you might one day find it useful to refer to, if you do ever do any serious writing.

If I get to New York on my way to or from Jamaica, I'll try and telephone you from there—but, still, I don't know even if I'll get off my Holwell-London tramlines.

Have a wonderful time. Thinking of you a great deal.

Every scrap of love and a large consignment of kisses. Will you give my love to all the Edwards too.

Your devoted
Pa

From 1959 I attended a private progressive co-educational school near our home. I continually received bad—'lazy'—reports; all of which evoked stern lectures from my father and promises on my part to 'work harder'. I succeeded in avoiding any strenuous mental effort until the year before my 'O' levels—and would probably have continued to do so without this gentle ultimatum. It did have a very strong effect, and the following summer—to everyone's astonishment—I passed my 'O' levels.

*Gurneys,
9 April 1964*

My dear Mandy,

I think it might be better if I write to you, rather than talk to you, about your report. It is not an altogether bad report. But it is not good enough, and not as good as I had hoped it would be in the light of the talk we had together at the end of the previous term, when you assured me that from then on you would be making an all-out effort. Now I am writing because I love you so much and also know you so well, and therefore for your sake want to try to emphasise certain points. Please read this carefully—and *think* about it.

First, I think I can justifiably expect you to agree that I am not anti-fun, anti-TV, anti-pop-records, anti-Beatles, anti-boyfriends, or anti- any of the exciting and enjoyable parts of being a teenager with lots of friends and lots of attractions outside schoolwork. I, and Mummy, want you to have a happy, full and varied life, and you have a lively mind and an eager nature that quite understandably wants to express itself in all manner of directions. I also recognise that you and I are very much alike in temperament, and patience and self-discipline aren't our strongest characteristics. So I do, from within myself, know something of your difficulties.

But its also because I do myself experience these difficulties that I feel I can more strongly put these points. Now these may seem rather boring and obvious things to say, but they are true and have to be said.

As a TV commercial might phrase it: 'There's no substitute for work'. What I mean is, that there are no short cuts—you have to work for what is worth having. But also, and this is much more important, it's in work that the greatest satisfactions lie—the satisfaction of stretching yourself, using your abilities and making them expand, and knowing that you have accomplished something that could have been done only by you using your unique apparatus. This really is at the centre of life, and those who never orientate themselves in this direction are missing more than they ever know.

Unfortunately, perhaps, but inescapably nevertheless, you and every child has to fit into the pattern. You have to subject yourself to the tests and assessments—in other words, you will have to take your 'O' and 'A' level examinations. You can, of course, scamp them and do badly at them, and in the long run you may well feel that it didn't matter much that you did. But knowing you as a person of pride and with a natural critical faculty and sense of values, I think you will regret that you scamped them, because you will always know that you didn't fulfil yourself.

I don't know what you eventually will want to do, of course. I am pretty certain that if you wished it, you could without much difficulty get to university, and very likely to Oxford or Cambridge. You may decide you don't want to do this at all, and that's not going to blight your career. But I also feel certain that you would both delight in this experience and get a tremendous amount from it, and that you would always be glad later that you did make the necessary effort.

The point I'm at last arriving at is this, Mandle: you must do two things. One, you *must* sort out your personal scale of priorities; you must tidy up what can be relegated as quite amusing, minor, occasional side pastimes—and by that I mean the Beatles, and pop records, and watching TV, and all the other alluring diversions; and you must, having done this, set yourself a new standard, which is to stick to your responsibilities of schoolwork and execute them thoroughly and with enjoyment and zest, and not try to push them out of the way as quickly and superficially as you can—or even not tackle them at all. In other words, you must from next term on resolve, firmly and decisively, that you are now going to give an entirely different performance—that you are going to make real use of the talent and potential that I know you have. You honestly haven't any more time for trying to dodge the issue, and I hope you will feel that you want to make a great effort of bringing a new attitude and determination to bear on your schoolwork.

It really is for your sake that I'm saying all this. As you know, I hate waste—and I especially hate to see a human being wasting ability and opportunities, because in a way this is a failure of one's duty as a human being, which is to enrich and strengthen ourselves and so the whole human race that we're bound up in, like it or not.

I can't, and certainly don't want to, go on every end of term repeating this kind of burdensome lecture—and in any case, it would be purposeless from now on. The reason I am writing to you at such length is because this is your last lap coming up before 'O' level, and you haven't any time left now to delay deciding how you are going to deal with the situation. If it was that you couldn't cope, or were unhappy at school, or simply hadn't the intelligence, one would accept that you might just as well do other things. But those aren't the facts, and I have to make this final attempt to make the situation clear to you: not only that you can do it, and probably exceptionally well, but that in the end *this is where you will find the greatest pleasures and deeper satisfactions are*—not from being browbeaten and nagged into working, but from doing it voluntarily and with an enthusiasm that will grow as you increase your capacity and knowledge. But you have to start off by disciplining yourself into a single-mindedness and a whole-heartedness that is still very much absent.

Will you let me know how you react to this?

All my love, darling daughter

Pa

My German grammar was so non-existent that my German master was reluctant to enter me for the 'O' level exam, convinced that I had no chance of passing. My parents, with their usual faith and determination, refused to give up, and sent me off (much against my will) to Heidelberg, under a paying-guest/ tutorial scheme.

My father, having completed research on his book 'The Bootleggers', was trying to get the text of it onto paper.

We had at that time a large number of pets, including a Siamese cat named Pyewacket, two peafowl, a neurotic bloodhound (with no sense of smell) called Sherlock, and several white doves.

*Gurneys,
14 April 1965*

Dearest Mandle,

We were very pleased to have your cards, and to know that you had arrived safely and are enjoying it there. So glad, too, that you successfully made contact with Eleanor M—how nice of her to take you to the opera. The weather there sounds to be better than here: in the past week it has turned dull and grey, and there was a fantastic hailstorm a couple of days ago, while today it's just drizzling drearily.

Cliff [Michelmore] is away today and Magnus [Magnusson] has now gone off to Norway filming, so I am in the studio every day, which is rather distasteful after all those free days at home. Mummy came up on Monday night, and we went to Desmond's wedding party; there was quite a large gathering at the house of Sir Robert and Lady Matthew, including a woman named Joyce Wright, mother of two St Christopher boys (do you know them?) I also talked to Patience a bit. They (Desmond, new wife and two children) were going off to Rome, but D isn't well (looks rather ill actually) and it was cancelled. We saw the Malberts at Codicote on Saturday night. The lamps are now fixed up on our terrace, on the grapevine lamp posts; I hope they look all right, but secretly suspect that it now looks like a filling station at the back there. Tristan went up to Cambridge yesterday to have lunch with the family of his new girl friend (No 147), Sarah, I think it is, and reappeared at Gurneys at about midnight.

Pyewacket misses you terribly. All he does is stalk on

his gawky legs all over the house, yowling and grumbling, and repeatedly goes up your stairs to see if you've sneaked back. All the other animals and humans are in good form, I think.

I do hope that by now your cold has gone, darling. I shall look forward to seeing you soon, but in the meantime have fun and do some work on your German.

Love and kisses
   Your adoring Pa

BBC,
20 April 1965

Dearest Poodle,

I got in today (Tuesday) for the first time since last Thursday—the Programme's Easter break—to find your letter (undated, so I'm not sure when it was written) awaiting me. Oh dear, darling, I'm so sorry you're not having a very enjoyable time, and that you're still not feeling awfully well. I do hope that was a temporary phase and that by now it's better all round. After your last card home, Mummy wrote to Frau H asking to arrange for you to have tuition at the University, so that you can get out and about a bit, and meet more young people. I do hope that by now something has been organised.

Actually, though you needn't feel that you're missing the lovely English spring. Easter was appalling here. Bitterly cold, and SNOW fell on Saturday: the rest of the time, just vile, icy sleet. Nobody really stirred out of doors. Your grandmother came over on Sunday and stayed overnight—she's not really at all well. The boys and I did a bit of spasmodic work on the farm when the weather permitted it. Actually we were working on Friday when the heavens opened and solid water lashed down. I've spent most of the time working on the book, trying at last, to begin putting words on paper: a traumatic moment. Tris bashed his car in, on the way back from seeing his new girlfriend in Cambridge. The peafowl are now being given their liberty. We leave the door open each morning, but such creatures of habit are they that they now barely poke their beaks out, and when they do they merely tentatively stalk around the barn and stand inside the garage all the time!

Nothing of any great importance or interest to tell you. We're dining in London with the Malberts on Friday, going to a party on Thursday, and going to a gathering for Norman Mailer, the American novelist, on Sunday. Oh yes, I'm moving out of my bedsit in Temple Chambers on Friday to this new basement flat in St John's Wood, so that's going to be a chaotic day.

Write again, love, and I do hope that by now you're a bit more attuned to it there, and not finding it too much of a drag.

Always all my love
Pa

*Heidelberg,
20 April 1965*

Dear Mother and Father,

Here is another letter. I have not been doing anything. Actually I have but I am still mad at you for sending me here (I TOLD you that I didn't want to come, didn't I?). All the English girls I meet are having such fun and going to so many places. I am so JEALOUS. I have not done ANYTHING ANYTHING ANYTHING with Frau H. If you want to know the truth (which you probably don't) I HATE it here. I went out today with some German and English girls, and I couldn't bear the thought of coming back here. Frau H is nice, I suppose, but if I was her daughter I wouldn't know what the outside world was like. She was horrified that a fifteen-year-old English girl staying near here had a steady boyfriend. So I told her I had two. She thinks I am so good and well-behaved; I wanted to shock her.

I enjoyed this afternoon. We just went to the zoo, but it was so nice to be with humans of my own age. I'm going to see one of the German girls again—and then write to her. Yesterday afternoon the two pupils of Eleanor M came over with their German girls. I'm going to a dance with them on Saturday but Frau H thinks I am 'so young' and 'strange men are not nice'. So her son has got to chaperone me. I don't like her son—and I'm sure he's queer.

I wish you would come to see me like you thought of doing once, because it will probably be the last time you see me alive—I will either die of boredom, drown in my tears or commit suicide. And when I'm in my coffin you'll be sorry you sent me away (I hope!):

*And when I'm dead and in my coffin
With my feet pointing t'wards the sun*

> *Come and sit beside me parents*
> *Come and look on the way you done*
> *(Adapted from Joan Baez)*

Well I suppose I'd better go now. I have written to Melanie Kingdom but I don't know whether to send the letter because I don't think Frau H likes me having visitors. Or going out. She says I can go dancing with her son. Ugh. Actually I'm beginning not to care what she thinks. I don't care if she hates me. I hate her. Please, Please write, or come, or something. Love—M

PS I WANT TO COME HOME. I am lonely bored and unhappy and frustrated and furious and of unsound mind and hysterical & ill & sick & dying and stupid and jealous and full of hate and angry and lonely (again) and fat and nasty and miserable and lonely etc.

Gurneys,
25 April 1965

Dearest Mandy,

All right my dear, we have taken your point: you don't like it there and wish you had never gone. Do you think you could now stop complaining about it and make up your mind to extract a little value out of the experience?

We have heard nothing from you about what the city is like, about where you have been (although you mentioned in passing that you had been to the opera with Eleanor, but nothing about what it was like or if you had enjoyed it), about your impressions of Germany and German living.

May I just try to get across to you that, although I'm sorry it didn't prove to be a jollier billet, and that you have found the surroundings irksome, I spent the money I have spent on sending you there because I wanted you to have an additional chance in your examinations. It wasn't just a holiday, so please try to adjust yourself to the situation and use it to benefit. I assure you it isn't either becoming or amusing to get this stream of abuse for having organised this.

All OK here. You're not missing any glorious weather. Here, too, it's been pretty indifferent, and we've had very grim, cold days of rain and hail.

It's a pity you can't get classes at the university. As you probably know, Mummy wrote only a few days ago asking for this to be arranged, but had the reply that it's now closed. In the meantime, try to understand that Frau H has quite a responsibility, having a teenage English girl with her, whom she must be sure is kept out of trouble, and she seems to me to be taking her duties seriously in making sure you come back with more German than you left with.

All love, your ever affectionate Pa

In the summer of 1965 both my parents set out across the States to research for my father's book on migrant workers, 'Hard Travellin'. They drove from the East Coast to California together then spent a few days with their friends there. My father then continued up and across the States while my mother returned to England. At the same time, my younger brother, in his turn, was going to California.

*Davis, California,
24 July 1965*

Dearest Kids,

I'm now 500 miles away from Mummy and the Edwards, and north of San Francisco, and having finished my business here, move on tomorrow up into Oregon to look at some lumber camps, and then I shall begin the rather daunting-looking return journey thru' the Northern states. I've just come up the San Joaquin Valley, just about the most fertile and productive agricultural valley in the world, with an interesting history of immigration, going right back to the bringing in of Chinese coolie labour in the 1860s, then successive waves of Filipinos, Italian and Portuguese, and Mexicans, and latterly Negroes and white Americans right across from the Southern States.

I *think* it's all going satisfactorily; I'm certainly amassing a good deal of material but I find it a bit difficult to be sure, until I draw back from it and try to assess how it'll all jigsaw in, just how relevant it all is. One thing I've discovered: the hobo may be officially extinct, but actually is alive in large numbers, still riding the freight trains, still down on the railroad tracks, still drifting on from hobo 'jungle' to hobo 'jungle'; I've talked with quite a few of them, the spoil of a society that still very wastefully mines its human material, the kind of by-product of a nation still very much in transition between settlement and stability. The actual physical process of covering the itinerary I set myself is fairly demanding: the huge distances to be covered, then the finding of people and situations, the interviewing and note-making, the transcription in the motel room in the evening. I miss Mummy very much because she was sharing in all this routine work, and also of course doing some of the driving, but, more important, providing good companionship. I rang her up this morning and shall do so again before leaving tomorrow and before she catches the New York plane. We had a tremendously nice time at the Edwards: they are such nice people. The weather there is marvellous now, brilliantly sunny but not over-hot, and there's the pool always there to plunge into when the notion takes you.

I've just been totting up that I've done 4,442 miles so far, although of course that's only about half. The Ford has up to now run in a very stalwart fashion: no breakdowns at all, touch piles and piles of wood. The only possible near trouble was when, late in the afternoon on my way up from the Edwards, I was doing a steady 80 mph along the freeway, and suddenly there drawing in front of me was a highway patrol car with its stop light flashing. The cop, however, proved very fascinated by my international driving licence, and asked what I was doing in the States, and then entered into a long chat about the subject of the book and finally said he'd decided to let me off with a warning instead of booking me for a $60 fine—and said he'd very much like to have a copy of the book when it comes out!

The Beatles are due in Los Angeles late in August, and Herman's Hermits just before them—both are getting heavily plugged on the radio. But really there isn't much interest in pop music here; records are played all the time, but just as fillers between the commercials and there isn't the kind of keen attention paid to the top ten, etc., that there is in Britain. One record that's being played a lot here is by Bob Dylan 'Like a Rolling Stone'; I don't know whether or not that's been released in Britain or whether it's on one of the albums we have, but I do like it enormously. The Edwards family had never heard of Bob Dylan, and barely of Joan Baez; I tried to convert John to listening to the Beatles, but I don't think successfully. We went into a club down on Sunset Strip, in Hollywood, one night, where there was quite a good group, with rather short long hair, ersatz Rolling Stones, called The Enemies, who were playing a lot of Beatles stuff. John Edwards takes it for granted that anyone with long hair is a delinquent shit-carrier.

Well, how are you lot? I think of you often and miss you all a great deal. I hope you got the money Mummy telegraphed OK, and that you've been managing to cope without any difficulties. It seems still a very long time before I shall see you all again, but we'll have a grand reunion when we're all once again foregathered at Gurneys. I get a tremendous amount of interest out of travelling, especially out of America, but it never fails to strengthen my gladness that I live in England and that I have Gurneys and my children to return to.

Do take care of yourselves. With fondest love
Pa

Ypsilanti, Michigan,
5 August 1965

Dearest Mandy and Tris,

Have just got into Ann Arbour—or rather, haven't got into Ann Arbour, because I spent a tedious hour trying every hotel in the town, and finally had to drive on here to get anywhere. So I shall have to drive back tomorrow to the university. Chicago worked out quite well; made contact with old Wobblies, and got good stuff from them; also some Mission stuff; finally, by wiring him, got in touch with Nelson Algren, and spent the evening in one of his sleazy haunts: enjoyable.

I also rang Fabian. He had arrived the day before, but hadn't had the letter I posted off well in advance to be there awaiting him: the U.S. mail is the lousiest in the world.

The journey since I left Los Angeles has been very eventful and full of interest, but I'm deeply thankful it's nearly over: these long endless days of hurling along are pretty killing: and after hunting up material in South Dakota, I virtually abandoned Nebraska and Iowa, for time was short and I felt pretty used up, and I just got across as quickly as possible those vast and rather dull land-distances. Frankly I don't think I'll even try for the up-state New York farm-workers I was going to talk to. I feel at the moment I've had a bellyful of migrant workers. I thought I'd try to talk to some trucking companies in New York, and the drivers, and get some dope on internal flying.

I do hope that things are organised at Gurneys and

that by now Mummy's home and settled. Take care of her and yourselves.

All Love. Pa

PS. I had two curious dreams: 1. That I walked into the gate of Gurneys and Pyewacket saw me, rushed forward, paws held wide like arms, leaped up on me, and SPOKE: he said 'Hello darling', the 'Hello' being a kind of extended miaow. 2. That my father had been staying down at Gurneys, and when I walked out to inspect the vine I found that he'd cut it right down to the ground and pulled all the branches off the canopy as he said he thought it would look tidier.

After the end of my 'O' level year, I spent my first holiday away from my parents—with three friends in a caravan in Dorset.

Gurneys,
2 September 1965

Dearest Darling Me,

Thank you for your nice letter and card, and we were happy to hear that the caravan is Hilton-like, and that you're having fun, finding lots to do and meeting some nice people.

Much as ever here. I've just (4.30 pm) got back from the second day's filming at Henlow RAF Camp, which is to be for the BBC's Battle of Britain anniversary programme on September 13. They'd managed to gather together from all over Britain a rather marvellous collection of old crates, going right back to a 1912 Blackburn. (I'm finding it almost impossible to type, because Tillie, after whining heart-brokenly on the floor, is now on my knee, and her poor retarded little one-cylinder brain can't understand that I am trying to type a letter to you, so she constantly rests her head in the crook of my elbow and makes me go idu89d9d)(-.?£–£4dddyxxofpgph("'/oxD if you see what I mean.)

I had to interview four pilots, including Flt. Lt. Ginger Lacey, who, as a young sergeant pilot, was the top scorer of the Battle of Britain, with eighteen German planes on his record, and also a Colonel Von Schroetter, a very Hunnish hun, in a Goering-like uniform, tall hat, who kept obsessively saluting everyone and clicking his heels, who flew Junker 88s against London. The interesting point both made is that during the Battle of Britain, which was of course one of the most crucial battles of all time, neither had any idea he was involved in anything of particular significance: it was just part of the general pattern of duties they'd got embroiled in.

Just found in the garage, a WHITE WING; so obviously that goddamned, sinister, satanic killer-cat Piesie has assassinated yet another pigeon, and an all-white one at that, curse his insatiable bloody fangs.

I've been working hard at the book and have written about 12,000 words, or at least, 12,000 are down on paper, although of course a great deal of cutting back may have to be done.

It's terribly spectrally quiet in the house without you all, really quite morbid. I hate it without you around, and the sounds of two transistors each individually on Radio Caroline and Radio London, and the record player simultaneously grinding through a pack of 45s, while you conscientiously work away at your school books, ignoring Sherlock's moaning, Tillie's yapping, the telephone ringing, the peafowl crowing, Mr Peters roaring up and down with the motor mower, Mummy's Sacred Washing Machine munching noisily with its metal jaws at yet another sacrifice of my best cashmere sweater, and Mummy on her knees and touching the tiles with her forehead singing incantations to its Divine Goodness and Omnipotence... all the usual country peace and stillness.

We went to London last night, to an Encounter party at Mel Lasky's, which was enjoyable: its three months about since I was last in London, and the London life, but actually I so much prefer being down at Gurneys, and could, had one not to earn filthy disgusting money, be perfectly happy pottering about here, writing quietly away at books. Why can't one ever do what one WANTS. Take care of yourself, dearest Poo, and longing to see you soon.

Your loving Pa

I began my first 'A' level year in September, taking French, German (after a good 'O' level pass) and English.

My father worked in London most of the week and stayed at his pied à terre, *in St John's Wood.*

St John's Wood,
27 September 1965

My dearest daughter,

Mummy has shown me the list of books you need for 'A' level—that's quite a formidable battery, but, it seemed to me, not by any means dreary and dusty, but all of them interesting fields. We'll get you those you've put down. In the meantime, I've been going through my shelves, and found some you need and also others that I think you'll find relevant and useful in their own right:— Grierson and Smith's 'History of English Poetry' have quite a lot of Hardy and Yeats, and there's also here 'Selected poetry of Yeats'—I'll get you the complete poems, but this will be something to be going on with. . . . I don't have much on German or French literature, but Mario Praz's 'The Romantic Agony' is fascinating, provided you can cope with his long quotes in the native language (he makes the familiar erudite presupposition that we all speak fluently at least three foreign languages). All these I'd eventually like to have back in my reference library, but do keep them as long as you need them.

The others are Orwell's 'Essays', which I'm certain you'll relish just to read, apart from the necessity of having to study them. Orwell had, in my view, one of the best critical minds of this age—a keen shaft of light cutting through every subject he looked at, the viewpoint, of course, of a socialist, but a totally independent non-party socialist. He also wrote with such bony no-nonsense clarity. What will be particularly of value to you is Orwell on Yeats, but 'Inside the Whale' (an appraisal of the intellectual's position in the era of totalitarianism) is exceptionally good. 'A Hanging' and 'Shooting an Elephant' are anti-imperialism from the angle of a man who was involved in it—after leaving Eton, Orwell went into the Burmese Police, and it was there that he first experienced the disgust and horror he gradually crystallised towards the old order of empire-building, and that made him both a socialist and a writer.

On the Wall Street Crash, 'Only Yesterday' is a very entertaining bit of contemporary journalism, not enormously profound, but it'll give you the outlines. Also 'The Aspirin Age' has some very vivid and fascinating stuff on that period, especially The Crash chapter. . . . These two books are rather valuable to me, especially as they're difficult to obtain now, so do be sure I get them back eventually. Do hope to be seeing you soon. Look after yourself.

All love from your affectionate Pa

My school was principally a boarding school, though I and a few others went as day pupils. Most social events went on after school hours, and at the end of each term the social life increased. Most of my friends were boarders; and in order that I could join in the end of term festivities, I used to spend the last few days of each term staying at the school, sleeping in the sickroom.

At home we had acquired a new kitten and four chinese geese.

Gurneys,
5 December 1965

My Dearest Mandle,

The news may have filtered through to you that I've been at home this past couple of days with vague gastric 'flu, or some similar blight; anyway I spent the whole day in bed yesterday, and am now up and feeling improved, tho' still not exactly lusty. Mummy has gone up to London today to try and demolish a bit of Christmas shopping, but she has just telephoned to say she's on her way back early to avoid the journey after dark, as the fog there is still very bad.

I drove to Cambridge and back on Sunday to give the talk to the young men of St Catherine's College, and it was a very nasty drive indeed—no fog, but a glassy coating of ice on the roads. It was quite an enjoyable evening, really, altho' I don't basically enjoy addressing audiences. After sherry in the room of one of the undergraduates, I was entertained to dinner at High Table, with all the dons, in Hall, and then did my stuff. There seemed to be quite a lively interest among them in journalism and television.

I had the very shocking news over the telephone from Liz Cowley at 'Tonight' just now that Xanthe Wakefield had killed herself. As you may remember, I worked with Xanthe on quite a lot of stories—she was a producer there, a brilliantly clever and nice girl, with a double-first at Oxford, daughter of a Tory MP; she had for a year or two been having rather an unhappy love affair, and a little time back had a nervous breakdown; and now, apparently, she last night took an overdose of sleeping pills. It seems such a terrible waste of life and talent.

How are you getting along? Is it bone-freezingly cold in your cell? Well, it'll be good training for any Arctic expeditions you may decide to go on. Oh, I forgot—another rather sad item of news was that Peter Small, one of the aqua-divers who was killed in California yesterday (they were attempting to get down below the maximum depth so far penetrated) was someone I knew quite well. He was assistant to the Picture Editor on 'Picture Post'—we never got on particularly well, but all the same it is disturbing when someone you know so well suddenly dies in this way.

I think everyone and everything here is all right. The new little kitten really is very sweet indeed—and I say this as a non-cat-lover. It's the funniest little blob of tawny fur—and I suspect it's only half cat and the rest lion. The geese are well settled in now, and waddle about trumpeting irritably if you set foot on *their* lawns.

I must now press on and try to write something for my 'Harper's' book column—goodness knows what, but I suppose something will emerge.

All love from us all here
    Your very affectionate Papa

*St John's Wood,
10 December 1965*

Darling Poodle,

Nothing of any importance or relevance to write about really, except that I do miss you all so much when I am imprisoned up here in London for days on end, and when I really want to be at Gurneys. Knowing what you are doing and hearing you talk about school and your friends, and what you're reading, and your grouses and your plans for the weekend, and all the ordinary daily talk are of much more interest to me than all the boring old politicians and 'people in the news' that my time is diverted to.

One thing I have been meaning to say, but will now, is how pleased and happy I am at the way you have been working and applying yourself in the past months. I know I am a fearful nagger, and far too often remark upon minor things that momentarily irritate me than upon the things that make me so proud of you. I think actually that the main reason why on occasions we've flown at each other and verbally battered each other is because of your spirit and determination, and what is important is to keep those things, and it doesn't matter a jot that they clash with my unreasonableness at times. They are part of the reason I love you so much (apart from the fact that you've got alarmingly pretty in the past short time) and this is vital in being a person in your own right: to declare yourself with certainty and to stand up against disagreement and argument for what you believe to be true.

Isn't it sad about the peahen dying, or rather, sad

about the peacock, now alone in that big barn. I don't really know what to do about it. We must have an inquest. I must return to Lime Grove, where all my waking hours seem to be spent, but will be seeing you in a couple of days (Friday's off, I hope)

Your loving Pa

The following Easter I returned to Heidelberg, to stay with a German girl I had met on my previous visit, and once more to attempt to improve my German grammar.

My younger brother, on the brink of his 'O' levels, was sent to a family in France to improve his French.

BBC,
6 April 1966

Dearest Mandle,

How are You? It was nice to hear you on the telephone, and to know that you'd arrived safely and were settled in with Karin. How does Heidelberg look after your time away? Is the weather nice there? Are you managing to get any tuition at the university? I do hope you've happily picked up the threads and are enjoying yourself—and learning more German.

We've had a bit of a crisis over Fabian and his stay in France. After seeing him off on the train in Paris, Mummy got back to London on Friday night, then spent the next day shopping and went on to the theatre. During the afternoon I had a call from Margaret Benenson, who had been trying to contact Mummy in the country. It was to say that this two-bit Count, who was to be his host, objected to his hair and wanted him removed. As you can imagine, it was something of a problem, because of the tenuous communications, but eventually I got on to the agency in Poole, and they in turn managed over the telephone to find Fabian an alternative family, where, I hope, he has now transferred. I feel in such a boiling rage at this mean-minded despicable little bourgeois crum that I'd like to see him face to face—for it was a beastly thing to do to a young boy, and Fabian can't have felt anything but terribly unhappy and upset. The French really are the most unloveable people in the world, I think, with all the worst kind of meanness and conventional hardness of any. Anyway, the agency seems certain that this alternative place should be reasonable in atmosphere, and Mummy will be telephoning Fabian tonight.

No other news of especial interest. I shall be going down to Gurneys tomorrow evening. It looks a rather grey and wet prospect for Easter, but if the weather clears I think I may have a day out with George Evans, botanising and ornithologising, over at Flitwick Moor and that interesting country round Ampthill.

Do write love, and take care of yourself, and warm wishes to Karin and regards to her mother.

Your loving Papa

Between 1966 and 1968 the letters cease completely. The reasons are numerous. Some have been lost or destroyed in various stages of transit. But communication was, in any case, infrequent.

In 1967 we moved house, and the same year I left school after getting the necessary 'A' levels, and with a place at university for 1968. I lived at home until after the exams, and my father was at home more frequently than he had been; and so there was no need for correspondence.

In the summer of 1967, after my father's insistence, I joined the National Youth Theatre and spent the season in London, with frequent visits home, and meetings with my parents.

I continued to live in London during the Autumn, taking a typing course, which my father had decided would be invaluable to me. No doubt he was right but I loathed it, and left at Christmas.

At the beginning of 1968, I went to Rome as an au-pair. At about the same time, my father began to have kidney trouble, and went through a series of tests, which proved him to have a tubercular kidney. He was desperately depressed—he found physical imperfection intolerable, and the thought of his body giving out on him angered and frustrated him.

The day after he was told that he would have to go into hospital —with the possibility of a kidney removal—my younger brother was involved in a very bad car crash. I came home from Italy to help out. My father was not operated on, but was put on a course of curative drugs. He was ill for the whole summer, and in a state of intense, withdrawn depression.

In October I went up to University to study English and American Literature.

*Fleece House, Braughing,
15 October 1968*

Darling Mandle,

It was lovely seeing you last weekend, and finding you so well settled in. Both Mother and I were very impressed by the University itself, and happy to see that you're so comfortably installed in your room. We both hope it will be the setting for you for three satisfying and productive years.

We were a bit troubled by your telephone call this evening, and your own anxieties about your work— chiefly because it's very difficult at this distance to make useful suggestions and to give you a little comfort. We really do understand the disadvantage you're at in having done so little history, when probably most of your compatriots on the course have done it at 'A' level; on the other hand, you must remember that the University, when it took you, was perfectly well aware that you weren't highly qualified in this subject, but nevertheless saw you as the material they wanted. As I tried to indicate, off the cuff, on the telephone, I think your best way of tackling this problem is on the two levels: (a) make contact with other students who are doing the same course and get some help and guidance and tips from them and (b) ensure that your advisor does his job and advises you—put your problem before him firmly and emphatically and coolly and make sure that he appreciates your particular difficulties, and make sure that he helps you sort out the best way of tackling it. Even if you do find him in person not especially helpful, you might, again by making contact with others, who have him as their advisor, be able to get on better terms with him. Alternatively, if you simply can't get any aid out of him, don't just let it rest there and flounder—find someone who can, with authority, put you into better hands.

Now don't take all that follows as being 'preachy' but understand that I'm only saying it because I want to get you to save yourself unnecessary worries and depression. Absolutely for your own benefit you *must* keep before your eyes the fact of life that it is always to your advantage to make the pace—in other words, if you practice self-effacement, people are likely to take that at its value and just let you go on and efface yourself. In other words, you have to make your mark, and there's no one who will make it for you but yourself. So even if within yourself you feel you lack it, you must train yourself and make yourself more assertive and approach people and life with more self-confidence and assurance. The probably quite unfair truth is that people you'll come into contact with and work with and have relationships with won't bother to spare the time, to start with, to dig down and discover that you actually have talent and ability that you're masking or not making apparent. Don't sell yourself short. The way life works in its everyday mechanics is that people are likely to place upon you the value you place upon yourself, so it's up to you, without being overly aggressive, to make clear what qualities and capabilities you have. After all, what is there to be timid about? Any human situation is roughly one person dominating or making his presence felt upon the other. Why let them dominate you? If you shrink and let your voice fade away, then the cruel fact is that life will let you shrink and fade into invisibility. And you don't want to be invisible, do you? I really do realise and sympathise with the situation you're in, and know how confusing and daunting it must be to be thrust into this huge and amorphous and clever society—all the more reason for being determined to figure in it and not be swamped by it. What you must remember is that all sensitive and creative people go through precisely the same agonies and uncertainties—but those who excel and distinguish themselves are those who refuse to be pushed aside and stand firm. Mother and I both know perfectly well what your spirit is like and that you have the talent to shine— as long as you make the decision not to be washed under. The point is that everyone there, even those with A grades at History 'A' level, are still, secretly, going through the same doubts and uncertainty that you are— you're not alone or unique in that. So what you've got to do is come to the resolution to meet the problems face on and tackle them realistically—it's surprising how simply they can be solved if you take them to the right quarters and ask for assistance, rather than let them gnaw away inside you. You must know that Mother and I love you very much and want to give you all the help and support we can—but self-reliance and courage are things that no one else can supply: they have to come from within yourself. Just one other point: in having lived more than double the number of years you've lived, there's one truth I've learned, and that is that few problems, in perspective, and especially in restrospect, are worth the laceration and misery that they seem to bring with them at the time; it's quite amazing how trivial and unimportant the worst crises can appear after a passage of time. So try to be less perturbed by what seem to be pressing down on you from all directions—you'll find they've dissolved and gone after a few days or weeks or months. In other words, don't panic about life—take it more in your stride. But do be sure that you're determining where the stride is taking you and that it's you who are in control of it; and that very often means simply that you make use of advice and guidance available to you for the asking.

On an immediate and practical level, you have the advantage of knowing a few people there (which most of the freshers don't) so take that advantage.

Anyway, love, you'll be all right, I know, and these first weeks will suddenly stop seeming bewildering and alarming and settle into a manageable pattern—as long as you take the decision to be the manager of them.

Mother reminds me that we didn't leave you with any bread. So enclosed is £3 which I hope will cope with immediate necessities.

I was glad to hear that you're actually involved in the Dramatic Society—but again, don't just settle for crowd scenes if you see an opportunity of getting hold of something you can do as well as anyone else. It's a pity this is going to swallow up your weekends, so I do hope you can manipulate it to get home for a day or two in between.

Lots of hugs and kisses and loving wishes
   Your affectionate Pa

Fleece House,
29 October 1968

Dearest Mandle,

I was so glad to have your letter and all the news of life in its new setting and pattern. And I'm delighted that your initial panic and fear seem to have subsided, and that you are coping with—and actually enjoying—life. You obviously have a formidable task on your hands, and I know only too well (as you know I know only too well!) the drowning feeling one can get when confronted by such an ocean of books and reading and absorption and decanting of your own interpretations. The only way of tackling it (which again I don't follow too faithfully myself, although perhaps I do once I've ceased wallowing in despair) is to take it at a steady stride, a bit like a horse pulls a cart, just keeping your eyes on the road immediately ahead, and suddenly you find you've covered more mileage than you thought yourself capable of—and do remember (as I think I said in my last letter) that you are the one who must take the strides, and work out your own pace and your own direction.

I can see your point about the significance of houses in 'Howard's End'. I dunno. It's so long since I read it, but vaguely I would have guessed that Forster was looking at the values and quality of life of that period, and that Howard's End in itself symbolised some of the structure and stability of the kind of class he was dealing with? Yes? Or is that just an imposed value judgement?

Write when you can about what you're doing—your academic and non-academic activities, because I'm interested in all your doings.

Must now press on with my own work.
All love, as always
  Your affectionate Pa

Fleece House,
24 January 1969

My dear Mandy,

Fabian had thirteen birthday cards, including ones from all the family—except you. I think it is quite important to him, being remembered, as he is away from home, and I know he noted the fact that you hadn't bothered to send him one.

Furthermore, you've now been back at the University three weeks, and all your Mother has heard from you has been an immediate phone call and a hastily scrawled note, after she had troubled to write to remind you of Fabian's birthday etc. She has, for instance, not even any idea if you went to, and enjoyed, the Old Vic play, for which she bought you tickets.

I find this a troublesome letter to write. It isn't the first time I have had to prod you with the point that you should understand, without it having to be spelled out, that Mother's thoughts are always very much centred upon all you children, and it lowers her spirits when there are long silences. It may surprise you to learn that I, too, want to have regular news of you all, to know that you are well and happy. I don't feel that this should need stating, but apparently it does: that as a matter of courtesy, thoughtfulness and concern you ought to keep in regular contact with the family—and that includes your brother. One should be able to expect that this is regarded not merely as an obligation, but as a natural wish on your part to do so. And lack of time simply isn't an adequate excuse: a letter, birthday card or telephone call cannot consume vital minutes of your week.

I hope you *are* well, and that your life is proceeding satisfactorily.

My love, as always, Pa

In November 1968, my father was elected Rector of Edinburgh University. After his inauguration in February 1969, he took his job very seriously and spent a great deal of time travelling to and from Edinburgh.

In May he took up a one-term Research Fellowship at Merton College, Oxford.

*Merton College, Oxford,
27 April 1969*

Dearest Mandle,

It was a great joy to have your letter, and thank you so much for your good wishes and thoughts. I arrived here the day before yesterday packed to the roof with suitcases and cardboard boxes, having apparently transferred most of the library from the attic. However, one of the first people I saw was Mark Cousins, who produced a trolley and helped me cart the stuff across.

I've now unpacked and am settling into what is a slightly unreal but highly pleasant pattern, and I think I shall probably stay here for ever. My room looks out across Christ Church Meadows, to pasture beyond where cattle are grazing now in the rather damp milky light, and the Thames beyond that. There is a French window leading out into the Fellows' Garden, where limes are just coming into leaf, and wide expanses of lawn run up to the old city walls, or 'battlements'—a raised walk which looks on to the Magdalen tower and the groves of elms around. I have a large sitting room white panelled and a bit mildewed and shabby, but nice, and an adjoining bedroom. The record player is set up and at the moment is playing Goossens with Bach, and my scout has produced a kettle, and cups and glasses, so I'm all equipped for doing a great deal of work—although I can see that is going to be the struggle. A great deal of time seems to be spent eating, or preparing to eat, or coasting gradually out of the eating with port and Sauterne and various sweetmeats, amid the silver candlesticks. It's very seductive, especially when the sun is shining, and not compulsively inducive to work.

However, I am getting a lot of work done. Like you, I'm welcoming this chance of re-orientating myself to a more sensible routine. I was in bed and asleep by 11.30 last night and up this morning at 8 and feel all the better for having had a whole day to operate within. In any case I don't think it can fail to be an enormously interesting and valuable interlude in my otherwise idiotic life. Don't quite know when I'm going to get down to the actual reason for being here, and the research and reading for it. I brought with me several overdue commitments, including a 10,000-word appraisal of Harriet Beecher Stowe and Civil War literature for a new edition of 'Uncle Tom's Cabin', which I'm working on. I must also, while here, try to knock off the Penguin for Richard Mabey.

Is there any possibility of you getting over here during my residence? It would be so nice to see you and show you round.

I do hope that you are now settled in and that it's a happy and productive term for you. I'm glad you will be able to get home quite soon to see Mother. As I think you know, I feel a little worried about decamping in this way. She's been absolutely first-rate about it, in encouraging me in it, and being happy for me, but all the same it is going to be a rather desolate period for her and it will be a relief and a help to me if you and your brothers can see that she's not left alone too much or unthought-of.

That's a book I've been wanting to read: 'Manchild in the Promised Land'. I never succeeded in getting my hands on it. If it's yours, could you pass it on to me eventually?

After the HBS & UTC appraisal (delivery date May 1st, which gives me three days. Horrors) and the Penguin, I hope I can turn with more leisure to other tasks the main one being this tenuous idea of connecting 20th-century totalitarianism with 19th-century pastoral romanticism: the seeds of so much of the Nazi blood-and-soil philosophy, nature-mysticism, etc. Little more than a notion at present but it's amazing how ideas mesh together.

Every good wish for your own work, love, do try to come over and see me.

All love from
    Your affectionate Pa

Merton College, Oxford,
21 May 1969

Dearest Poodle,

It was rather nice not to have read your letter until returning here, as it was a sort of extension of seeing you and hearing you chatter on madly. Did you get the train? Were you in time for it? I returned to here next day, and since seem to have been doing nothing but deal with correspondence, which piles up in great drifts like Autumn leaves in the gutter if left for a few days: this evening I drive away once more, over to Wimbledon to spend the night with Mother at Pat's, as we are getting the morning train to Edinburgh, upon which after arriving there will begin a hurricane of dinners, receptions, brains trusts, conferences, BBC recordings, etc., etc., and endlessly etc.: oh dear. The idea of finding a haven for a few months was really illusory: everyone sniffs you out and the post with all its demands and pressures reaches out its long parchment hand and has you by the throat just as before.

I do understand all your intense feelings about university and the period you're going through, with all its enjoyments and problems. It brings to mind Auden's dictum or definition of education, which was something like 'A process to induce the greatest amount of stress without cracking', and I suppose that's what it should do, stretch the mind to snapping point, but permanently leave it expanded; the important course is to be sensitively aware of where the snapping point is, and not to push it beyond that. Anyway, I have infinite faith in your innate judgement of yourself and your capabilities: I think you're fortunate in having a sort of in-built gyroscope which, despite your manic tendencies, does instinctively give you your bearings and your balance. The only matter upon which it fails is to give you reliable guidance on how to use outwardly and in relationship to other people the inner confidence you have—as your tutor perceptively remarked. This of course is the point I've nagged you on ever since you began saying 'da-da', which is you must address yourself to others more firmly, more loudly, more urbanely, more measuredly. You talk so well and brightly, with much original thought, that it's a terrible shame that much of it floods past as a blur and a gabble to others' ears. Slow down a bit; speak up a bit. Life, superficially doubtless, runs on rough, quick assessments so it's preferable to impress yourself with clarity upon those you encounter. Amen.

Sor yew on the telly! Civilisation ends at East Anglia. Anyway, Kenneth Clark seemed to think you were an attractive and promising lot, even if you haven't yet painted the Sistine Chapel. I'm just playing the new Dusty Springfield LP (In Memphis): terribly nice and soully; I'm very keen on Dusty. The Hart Report on Oxford discipline is being much discussed here. One of the dons told me that 'Isis' put out a questionnaire, including the query: 'Would you want to sit on a commitee with dons?' One undergraduate replied: 'May I answer that with another question—Would I want to be buried alive?' The sun is suddenly shining: I must try to sneak out with some books.

It was lovely all being foregathered on Friday, and I'm glad I at last saw 'Hair'.

Take great care, love
    Always your affectionate, Papa

I was twenty on 23 May 1969. In June my parents held a large birthday party for me.

May 29 1969

Dear Ma and Pa

I just want to thank you for everything you've done for me—you sent me to a good school, helped me to go to a university, encouraged (even bullied) me to try for the Youth Theatre, and to go to London, and abroad, all of which have done a great deal for me. Most of all, you've given me a good, happy home, with love and THAT is the most important thing.

So I'm 20 now, and on my own, but I will never forget what you've given me so far. I've been very lucky, in having two parents of whom I'm proud not simply as parents, but as people. I hope I can live up to you and make use of all I've got from you. Thank you

With my love, Mandy

*Merton College,
Oxford.
11 June 1969*

My dear daughter,

It was a great joy to be with you at the weekend, among friends who've known you since you were a babe, and you now so pretty and blooming and (which makes me happiest of all) so rounded as a person. Your thoughtful letter was of great value to your Mother and me—to know that you feel in harmony with us. It's what parents always hope will be the enduring relationship with their children but there is no formula for achieving this because I suppose, every single case is an individual inter-reacting with other individuals and one knows how often that inter-reaction fails. It is deeply satisfying that you feel— as Mother and I do when we're not worried about one or other of you and your transitory problems!—that our family has organically grown well. Of course one can— and should—love someone who may not measure up to all one's objective criteria of excellence, but what a bonus it is when, as in the case of one's own children, one can see them developing qualities of good judgement, independence of mind and honesty. I have always felt that Scott Fitzgerald's injunction to *his* daughter could hardly be bettered: 'I want you to be among the best of your race and not waste yourself on trivial aims—be useful and proud.' But now that you are 20 and such a fine young woman I know that—unconsciously or not—that outlook is part of the person you are. I think, too, that this is largely true of all your generation. Detachedly I envy you all—I think most of all for your friendships. My generation was fragmented. So many died or were shattered in the war that the childhood and youth of those who came through are quite separate and remote. I once came across this description (can't recall where) of the Upbringing of Caterina Sforza, who lived at the end of the 15th century: 'Her education conformed to the humanist ideals—from the mechanical recitation of Latin verses to the earnest concern with *virtu*, that is, the shaping of a thoroughly educated person, adept in the art of reasoning with elegance, order and profundity.' That seems to me unchangeably true of what education should offer to the eager mind, but a precious part of the university experience you are having, and your schooldays too, is that you have been making, and are still making, friendships with those who will be your friends for life—a background which becomes increasingly important and valuable as one gets older.

Well, dearest Mandy, I am sitting here in the gardens in magical sunlight and leafy greenery, conscious of the hours and days slipping by even faster and nearer to the time when I shall have to leave behind this stolen time—rising sadness. It will be lovely to have you here for something like the climax. Just you and I will be the Allsops at the Ball. It is Tuesday June 24—please note. 10 pm–6 am but we are invited to earlier drinks so try to be here earlier. Can you arrive for lunch? We will go punting if so.

Always, all my love. Your Papa

Wear/bring your big floppy hat &/or boater, jeans, shades etc. I'm told the ball transforms in the early hours from formal to outrageous (Long gown first, of course): you can use my room for 'sitting out' and changing.

My father's father died on 9 November 1969, after a short illness, and this letter was handed to me at the funeral.

Fleece House,
9 October 1969

(This wasn't sent in all the disruptions, but, belatedly, here it is)

My darling Poodle,

As you already know, Grandpapa is seriously ill: the further news last evening was that he had had to be operated upon and his chances are now slight indeed. I wanted you to know that your message reached him and what comfort it brought him. He has been so intensely proud of you all and you have given him great pleasure in your life. That I am grateful for but not in a formal sense for I know that your concern arose naturally and spontaneously from the strong compassion and love that has always been so marked in you. You have inherited much of his fierce and affirmative spirit—'the Allsop spirit', he called it, but you have unnecessary doubts about yourself and your adequacy to be loved. You should not have these misgivings about yourself. You are an exceptional person, and a *person* complete in your own right and must not seek reassurance of a kind which is not of your own fastidious standards. You have no cause to doubt the love Mother and I have for you. In any case it is a belief in your indomitable and singular talent which you must never compromise for others' approval, but follow your own star.

Incidentally, it gave me great pleasure to know that you have now an accredited Press Card—that writing is becoming important to you. It isn't an easy following, but it is, I'm sure, *your* creative course. Don't be daunted by its demands.

I love you very much.

Papa

My father and I had been on stormy terms for some time—a series of quarrels and semi-reconciliations. I spent a weekend at home shortly after going back to University at the beginning of October. During that week we reached breaking point, quarrelled violently and refused to speak or communicate for some weeks.

BBC,
24 October 1969

My dearest Mandy,

Mother tells me that you have been talking with her on the telephone, and that you are less than happy about the state of our relationship with each other. Well, darling, so am I, and I wish very deeply that they could be better. I know quite well my own weaknesses and failings, and one of them is intractability, and I know too that I've not been especially outgoing toward you for some time. But, you know, this really hasn't been one-sided or perversely cultivated as a whim on my part, and (I believe, though you may disagree) it did not originate with me. For certainly a year you seem to me to have been determined to disencumber yourself of all of us, except in the most formal and cursory way, and to resent any interest in your life and your activities from us. I think it's a sad situation that there should be this rift between not only you and me, but also between you and the rest of the family, and I think we should try from both sides to eliminate it, so let me say what I feel about the situation, and I wish you would do the same.

First, I do understand that you need to be an independant person and to make your independance clear, and that is exactly as it should be—every child should, for the most healthy reasons, strike away from its parents and feel in charge of its own life. But absolute independance isn't an enjoyable or desirable state, for along with it go loneliness, and solitariness. The precious thing about a family, I believe, is that, without declaration of it and even at a distance, a member can feel the love and support of the others—but of course this does carry with it the obligation of reciprocity: it's a small unit of society in which you have to contribute your part as a member of that society. Of course I know that when the family closeness is claustrophobically overtight, this can be suffocating, and a very natural reaction might be to break free completely just to draw air. You may feel differently, but I don't think that this is true of ours. I've always liked to feel that we were, all of us, pretty relaxed while at the same time having a very warm centre, but Mother and I have always tried to see that all you children had maximum freedom, both of movement and of expression, within the limits of our concern for your welfare. The rejection that I feel you've made of us does seem to me disproportionate—to be more fitting with a situation in which a child had been more disciplined and governed than you were, and I suppose that's why I find your almost complete severance so saddening. You see, even when you have been at home on the past few occasions, you seem to have been in such a tense and hypersuspicious frame of mind, almost as if you were searching for accusations to make against us both; there may be many you can make, justifiably, but I truly don't think you have any cause to feel that we have ever tried to mould or suppress you—really, you know, the very opposite. I've always so admired your implicit talents and spirit, that if I've been guilty of anything it is of making you use them, of pushing you to realise yourself more fully.

Well, I imagine that you may have had enough of that and don't want any pressures brought to bear on you, and feel that you know best how to handle your life and your personal activities. I respect that and, indeed, as you've made it so harshly clear that you want neither comment nor advice, or even conversation, I felt that it could only exacerbate the not very harmonious feeling between us to try to offer any more, and so have deliberately left you alone. But you see, love, it seems to me that you also want a sort of passive, unquestioning silent approval of all you do. This isn't realistic about human beings. Any kind of relationship must involve an acceptance of people, and a pursual of that relationship, even when one or other concerned isn't at his best, or isn't necessarily in total agreement.

What I've felt has been so absent from your side has been any contribution, any relaxed, spontaneous warmth. If you find life unendurably unpleasant with us, well then you must stand completely on your own feet and say so, and not seek any more support emotionally: I still hope that you don't find it so, and that you can see that there is a completely viable way of remaining a member of the family to the full as an adult young woman. It's utterly normal and right that a child goes through a period of asserting himself, and in the process fighting off a lot of the old clinging remnants of the childhood relationship with his parents. Tristan went through a very detached phase for about a year (although not so painfully as you) and Fabian too in a different way; yet both, especially Tristan with his few extra years, has found a very happy rapprochement. I don't think he feels that we try to impose our ideas or rules upon him in any way at all, but I also think that he does value and trust our opinion and guidance, and he talks to me frankly and easily, but on a completely adult level, yet with the knowledge of the sure love there is between us and of my lasting involvement in his well-being and happiness. In other words, of course neither your Mother nor I expect—or want— you to relate to us in the way you did only a year or two ago. We want you to be free and in charge of your own life, but this needn't mean that you discard us. It's such a grievous loss for us all, such a needless waste of all the fun and companionship and sense of security that is one of the most important elements in a family. If there is this trust and love, then it should be possible for any person concerned to be honest—it all becomes a sham if your conditions for contributing to this relationship were to be just empty approval. If the bonds are strong enough they can take and withstand disagreement and even conflict: but it does seem to me that any hint of failure on our part to endorse everything you do (and even that to be done silently and negatively) is a sign for you to have done with us and home altogether.

Just one other point: I know you've now got a completely new circle of friends and activities, and I think you must know how pleased and glad I am that you're leading such a busy and successful life—it's just what I want, that you should be an individual with your own standards and taking your own decisions. So I certainly prefer this to a situation in which you might be so insecure and withdrawn that you were clinging fearfully on to the old safety of the framework you grew up in. Yet, again, there is a happy mean here, my dear, which would enable you to be in closer touch, by letter, than you are, and to be on good terms with us when you're home, which is a rare occurrence and fairly fraught when you are.

I do hope we can solve this. Mother is very miserable about the quickness of your resentment at any part she would like to have in your life—and yet feels that you expect a great deal of her, that you take but don't give. I wish you could feel that the giving doesn't entail being swallowed up by us, that we're really not trying to keep you in chains or alter you in any other way. You must know this in your heart, if you look back, that you have unbounded love from us. This sort of love isn't contingent upon any other love you feel for other people: it exists at a different level, and will always be there and need not monopolise your emotions: there's really no need to get rid of it to make room for the other.

My experience is that if one bottles up emotions or lets them go undiscussed, they can fester and unrealistically inflate within one. I don't really think there's all that impossible a blockage between us if it can be talked about—but perhaps you could simplify it by accepting all I've said as true, for I think that would clear up many of the divisions—I mean what I've said about my feelings for you as being true; I can't speak for yours, only hope that I'm right.

Always your loving Pa

Norwich,
26 October 1969

Dear Pa,

I was glad to get your letter—I've been wanting to write, but I am as uncompromising as you; and find it as difficult to 'back down'—which, I suppose, is what is behind my generally antisocial, antipathetic and horrid behaviour at home.

I think—or, rather, know—you exaggerate a lot in your letter, and a lot of it is both hurtful and untrue; I have not, for a whole year, determinedly and consciously been attempting to completely cut myself off from the family; nor do I deliberately and consciously create a harsh painful resentment of anything you and Mother do for me. I think you're deliberately choosing vehement adjectives, presumably to push home to me your view of my behaviour. Nor would I totally agree that I 'started it'—it becomes a vicious circle, in which I react against your reactions to me, etc. Nor do I agree that it's gone on for a whole year. After all, we've exchanged affectionate letters and been glad to see each other. I have, throughout this year, spasmodically behaved appallingly, but looking back I had believed that we were developing a good relationship (until recently) and find it hurtful that you don't think so. (But I think basically you do think so, and are simply emphasising the recent weeks.)

I hope you'll accept that. As you say in your letter 'If the bonds are strong enough they can take and withstand disagreement and conflict' so please *accept* my disagreement.

But I do know I have been behaving appallingly, reacting violently and cutting myself off. And I have been unhappy. I think it's a lot to do with adjusting to various situations at university

—and, as so often happens, when going through difficult periods, it's so much easier to take it out on people you're close to, and not explain the problem.

I don't have a problem as such. I feel I wasted a lot of my first year in endless and totally useless self-analysis; and missed out on a lot of other opportunities. I'm just following the crowd. We seem to do it—this miserable introspection—because everyone else is doing it. There's no one to turn to for help with real or imaginary problems, so I come home and take it out on you. I don't want to take and not give; I know how mother feels, and feel terrible because I do love her, and you.

Anyway, I hope I've changed—in general. I'm enjoying my work more, becoming (I think) more outward looking—and I'm terribly aware of you and ma. I'll be home in a couple of weeks so you can judge for yourself.

I'm sure that living out of residence has something to do with it (changing): not being surrounded by infectious neurosis. And living in a house, being more self-contained, and self-reliant; you begin to choose your friends—you have to decide whom you really do care about because access is less easy. Its also easier to organise yourself, and life becomes more controlled, and less chaotic.

I have an essay to write now, so must go. But I will be in touch and look forward very much to seeing you.

With lots of real love—Mandy

*Fleece House,
29 October 1969*

Darling Mandle,

Just got your letter upon returning from Edinburgh and thank you for writing so warmly and responsively. It makes me very happy that we can talk so openly to each other still because it shows that there's nothing fundamentally or permanently wrong between us. I think you see yourself and your adjustment problems clearly and honestly—just as I'm sure we can come closer again, because I understand far better how you've been feeling; —So my love, let's both try to put all this behind, mutually forgiven and forgotten. So glad your work is going so well *and* enjoyably. Thank you most deeply for keeping in such frequent contact with Grandad—it does mean so much to him.

Hoping to be seeing you soon.
Always your loving
Pa

The following letter was prompted only by general anxiety and not by any particular incident. The drugs debates were reaching their height and university was commonly considered central and conducive to drug-taking.

*Fleece House,
24 January 1970*

My dear Mandle,

I've just been reading *The Immediate Experience*—an excellent collection of writings on the pop culture (movies, Theatre, comics etc) which I think you'd be very interested in: do have a look at it—by Robert Warshow, an American critic who died a few years ago at only 37. It has an introduction by Lionel Trilling in which he describes how his friendship with Warshow developed out of their shared reaction against the prevailing notions of totally permissive, over-submissive parental anxieties to be pro-younger set at all costs, falling over backwards to be buddies with one's child on his terms, in other words leaving a void where perhaps there should be a pattern of principles, not to be die-stamped upon the young person, but there as a reference point. Anyway, Trilling in the course of this says: 'We confessed to the most retrograde desires for our sons, that they should become men of firm and responsible character; and adventurous, even heroic, in their quest for happiness and even for pleasure; and into the bargain, intellectually distinguished. We went so far as to think that we had the right to influence them to have such intentions for themselves; we were willing, God forgive us, to commit the ultimate sin of "putting pressure" on them.' That seems to me as good a summary as I have ever seen expressed of what a father would want for his child.

This brings me to the point at issue. I don't know whether or not you have encountered any sort of drugs. I do know that the opportunity for flirtation or deeper involvement—with the drugs scene arises easily in the university environment. I am banking my trust in your balance and good sense, and I hope that you reciprocally will realise that I have balance and good sense in my understanding, and shared interest, in the whole pop culture environment of which drugs, like it or not, are undeniably a part. I don't want to go into the complicated arguments for and against the degrees of acceptance of the varieties of drugs because, although this is intellectually worth doing, it would be likely to be inconclusive in that we might disagree about the levels of damage they entail. What I do want to do is put before you the *facts* involved and I ask you to examine them with care.

1. If you have already used, or have intentions of using, pot or any other illegal drug, as the law stands you are breaking it. If you are caught doing so the consequences will be that you will be arrested, charged, brought into court, and, if found guilty, sentenced—which could mean prison or a corrective institution. Even if it was no more than probation it would mean that for the rest of your life you would have this round your neck: you would have a criminal record. Apart from the immediate effect upon your career and future, your suitability for *any* job would for ever be damaged in the eyes of an employer. This is not being melodramatic: it is the flat truth.

2. Even if you haven't used or carried drugs and have no intention of so doing you must recognise that you can put yourself in danger of being *accused* of doing so by the places you frequent and the company you keep. I don't think the stories of police planting drugs on the person of someone they decide to take in—because, however innocently, he is one of a circle they decide to jump on—are entirely invented. You could find yourself in all the troubles described above, with the double misery of it not even being legally just.

3. Well, there you have the pragmatic, non-moral case against experimenting in these areas. But then there are

the moral/ethical/medical arguments. If you read that article I did on the subject in the 'Spectator', you will remember me saying that although I'm perfectly willing to concede that there may be levels of perception, etc, to which drugs give access, my mature (if mature only in the sense of age and a quite wide experience of the world) decision for myself is that a good mind and a civilised and rational attitude to life and standards of behaviour depend ultimately on clarity and discipline of thought— and, by their very nature, drugs are the very antithesis of these. Drugs must always be, by their nature again, an escape from reality and are resorted to by people not strong and resolute enough to deal with life on the terms they impose upon life. They are defeated, weak, lost and frightened people. I'm not proposing to go into discussion about how harmless or not pot is, or whether or not there is any direct correlation between pot and eventual use of heroin. Personally I'm inclined to think that causal effects here are probably overstressed. But what I am in no doubt about whatever is that once a person begins mixing in a drug environment, in which *all* drugs have an atmosphere of acceptance, then the really destructive ones are more easily drifted into. Indeed, the point inevitably comes when that person is confronted with the decision whether or not to go along with his social group: it becomes a testing point. He loses face and status in the eyes of his chosen friends if he holds out, and most people value the opinion of those immediately in their circle, so, if they want to stay in that circle, accept its standards and habits. Therefore this kind of environment is best stayed clear of.

4. This is purely the personal level. I've been delighted at how, suddenly and admirably, you've matured and found your feet as a person in the last year or so—to have found a composure and confidence you didn't have before, and I'm also tremendously pleased with the responsible and energetic way you're now tackling your work. Our personal relationship, and yours with the whole

family, seems to have reached a very happy state of easy and harmonious closeness in which we can talk—and disagree—with each other with openness and good humour. It's for this reason that I feel that I can write to you as I'm doing now. Of course as a father I have my own conception of principles and standards by which life can most satisfyingly be lived, and which I would like you, and your brothers, to accept and follow; but one of those principles has always been to trust your qualities of character and good sense to guide you without authoritarian rules and commands being issued by me.

For all I know the whole of this letter may be totally unnecessary, because maybe you have been so guided from within yourself. But read it over again before I next see you. I hope you'll understand it's written out of the greatest love for you.

Your ever affectionate Pa

For some time my parents had been thinking of moving as far into the country as was feasible for my father's work in London, and had been looking at houses. In November they found a Mill House in Dorset which seemed delightfully perfect. At Christmas, we all went down to look at it, and were all equally entranced by it, and its setting.

Fleece House,
5 March 1970

Dearest Mandle,

Merely a few words to say I was thinking about you this evening and to send greeting and salutations, etc.

There was a reference on the BBC news this evening to the sit-in at Kent, and I wondered if Tris was among their number. I'm up to here with sit-ins; much ado at Edinburgh about the retribution and vengeance being visited upon those who sat-in, not to say bust-in, at the Appointments Bureau, and then 2 days ago there was another outbreak of in-sitting, when a new wave of insurrectionists invaded the Old College and occupied the old building here. It is my contention that this is the feedback from the previous allocation of sentences by the Disciplinary Committee—suspended expulsion, plus up to £40 fine per student, which seems to be pretty harsh.

Mother and I got back last evening from Dorset, where we had 3 active days. You will, I think, be glad to hear that it seems we're within a hair of owning the Mill—contracts SHOULD be exchanged on Monday. Then, if it goes as the Jameses wish it to, we shall have to move out of here before Easter, in less than 3 weeks! This is an extremely unnerving prospect, as there's no hope of getting anything very effective done to the house before then. We spent Monday and Tuesday seeing 3 separate lots of builders on the spot and combing through the ruin with them in fine detail. By the time the 3rd one was at the beginning of his tour, the words suddenly choked in my craw—I couldn't repeat the litany again, and I despicably mumbled that I had to see someone at the cottage, shoved the papers into Mother's hands and split.

It was beautiful there. The weather was icy cold, and brilliantly sunny. As I stood on the edge of the leat, trying once again, vainly, to unravel its untangled mysteries, a dipper flitted onto the hatches, bobbed around a bit, and flew off—rather nice, for the uncommon and remarkable little bird, which as you may know, actually walks on the river bed to hunt for its food.

The general dilapidation stands out more markedly now that the house is bare of furniture. If we don't go broke it will be super.

Are you all right, love? I do hope that work is going satisfactorily, and that, tensions withal, life is reasonably happy.

All love
Papa

My parents moved into the Mill over Easter, 1970, amid the chaos of builders and decorators. They spent several weeks living virtually in the kitchen, the only habitable room, all furniture and packing cases sat stacked in the outbuildings, while the floors in the house were pulled up and relaid. I stayed in London to work, and to avoid the confusion.

*The Mill,
West Milton,
19 May 1970*

Dearest Mandle,

I stayed up all night last night, and now, at 2.30, my legs are buckling. It was an idiotic thing to do, really. After dinner, I returned to my study and carried on emptying packing cases and trying to get the shelves in order and throwing away rubbish and reassembling files etc, and when Mother went off to bed at about 10.30 pm I felt I simply couldn't get up and face another day of this sordid chaos, so I just went plodding on, without even sitting down, for the next eight hours, and eventually crawled into bed at 6 am. Then I was awakened (and forced out of bed) by men hammering at masonry and priming paint off my bedroom window. Still, I think the room needed that sort of relentless attack. It's much more under control now although there are still heaps of boxes to be unpacked.

Weather's sort of patchy here, but the countryside is incomparably beautiful. The wild flowers are surging along the hedge banks; ragged robin, lords and ladies, bluebells, hankbits—a blaze of colour. In our marshy meadow we've got a huge colony of marsh marigolds, which almost burn with yellowness. The dippers are nesting under our bridge! Haven't found the nest, but when Fabe was here two days ago I was taunted into going into the swimming pool (my limbs went blue with cold and I felt as if I'd been pumped full of anaesthetic but I did swim—Fabe chickened out, standing whimpering and whining on the side). We also threw Galadriel in

—she hated it—and I went on crutches along the yew walk, and saw the dipper flip out from under the bridge. Then its mate came whizzing along with a beak full of food. I scrambled down into the stream and waded about on crutches, but couldn't find the nest. But rather super, isn't it, having dippers nesting in one's garden? Yesterday Mother and I were driving back from Bridport and the other side of Bridport I saw a farm dog worrying something in a field of corn, so I stopped and climbed the barb wire and chased it off—it was a leveret. I brought it back to the car and nursed it all the way back to the Mill, but although it was still alive it was too badly torn under the belly (and bleeding over me profusely) so I had to drown it in the leat.

Thank you so much for your long and interesting letter. Your meditative experience sounds fascinating: the long, slow breathing is very much a central part of yoga, isn't it? Isn't it claimed that the masters can carry this to the point of suspended animation (and, with it, the spiritual which is their objective)?

Thank you very much, love, for what you have to say at the end of your letter. The test of real bonds between people is if they can continue to feel for their kith and kin the same strength of love whatever the circumstances.

Do let's see you again as soon as you can manage it. Take great care of yourself.

    Always your loving Pa

PS Four young dippers perched on the car tonight—just fledged.

I had been considering applying for the post of Editor of the University Newspaper. The job would have coincided with my final year.

The Mill,
20 June 1970

Darling Mandle,

I have just been talking on the phone to your Mother, she very much enjoyed her visit to Norwich and her time with you. She got back to London safely, and is staying with Pat in Wimbledon overnight.

She tells me that you are considering reversing your decision and trying for the post of Editor of the University newspaper. It would indeed be satisfying and seductive to be sought-after; I think you know that I have found your move towards journalism pleasing, so you will understand that I am moved only by objective considerations when I feel I must give my earlier advice on this a three-line whip, which is that I do seriously believe you should, regretfully, refrain. I can see that it must be tempting, and not a little frustrating to turn down this opportunity. But you have to weigh your priorities now and this final year is decisively going to determine what degree you get. I am sure it would be self-deception to argue yourself into believing that you can do both: make of the paper the excellent production you would wish to make of it *and* bring off a good pass. The second ought to take precedence. You must, I am sure, for what is going to be of long-term importance to yourself, hold to your decision. As you say, you can't live wholly in blinkers, but I do know from my own experience that a better way of stimulating one's concentration on academic or writing work is to make the contrasting activity, the diversion from it, a physical one. Shifting from one form of overdrive at the desk to another form of overdrive at the desk, will exhaust you. You have to feed your brain cells with blood and oxygen, and something like cross-country running, karate, hopscotch, Yoga or tiddlywinks even would be a better balance—quite seriously, do give a thought to doing something which will keep your body in trim, to aid and supplement the mental drill. When a Trinity hearty invaded Waugh's room at Hertford to demand tipsily and belligerently what he did for the college, Waugh replied that he drank for it. But then, Waugh only got a fourth.

You'll be 'coming down' soon, won't you? Have you thought about a summer job yet? Presumably you'll want to spend some time in London as you'll probably work there; but it would be very nice if you could take some time off and get down to the Mill for a bit.

Ever your affectionate Pa

In October I began my last year at University. I fluctuated for a while between anxiety and indifference over the Final Examinations, and occasional worry about future employment.

Fabian had finished his year's pre-diploma course at Camberwell Art College, and was about to begin a three-year Diploma course at Leeds Art College. Tristan had graduated from Kent in the summer and was looking for work.

*The Old Millstone,
17 October 1970*

Dearest Mandle,

I'm sitting out on the balcony typing this in blissful unwavering sunshine as it has been since morning; not, now, quite so hot but with a rather wan warmth and an over-ripish light in which the apples glow like red fairy lights and the hedges beyond the orchard are ablaze with haws and hips and have clusters of purple bruises which are blackthorn fruit. The Knoll's got a faint haze over it, like butter muslin, and all the trees straggling up it are flecked with rust; a general air of decline and fall but with an acrid smell of coming frosts in the sickly decay. We ran the leat through this morning to scour it out of autumn leaves, and Tris has built a new waterfall system down the side of the bank which began collapsing where the overflow pipe had eroded it with the constant trickle. The five barred gate has now been painted by Tris, and also most of the barn doors, and it all looks most bright and spic.

Mother and I were a couple of days in Bristol. I had to be there on Wednesday to run through commentary I've written for a film for the Natural History Unit there, so we stopped overnight and drove back yesterday morning. In the canteen a nice chap came over who proved to be Jim's brother-in-law, and who now has the Radio Bristol operation running for real since 5 weeks ago. He asked about you. Tris has now heard that he has to go through the formal procedure of applying for the Bristol job, so of course, there's no telling whether he'll be taken or not. He had an interview at Southern TV last week and appears to have got on well there. But there's no actual job going—just an interview on spec in the hope something will break before long. It's a bad time for getting into television: contraction and cutback on all sides; even with the BBC the order is that the butter—or margarine—has to be spread thinner, so when a new programme is starting it has to recruit from other programmes, which have to make do with fewer people. I do hope he gets in, and soon, because I know he will be a natural for a production job. We've had a letter from Fabe from Leeds, and spoken to him once on the telephone, and although I think he's found it a bit daunting to start with, I'm sure he'll have settled in by now. I think, too, that he's managed to find some less squalid lodgings. The Italian Embassy have now come up with the details of how he could have gone to study in Rome! That was the result of George Armstrong's kind enquiry. Still, it'll be worth keeping in the bag.

Lovely to have your long, informative letters, love, and we're so glad that everything is meshing and going along at a nice clip. It's good to know that you're enjoying your work and finding yourself so fully engaged with it. Have you definitely made up your mind that it *is* publishing you want to go in for, rather than journalism, say, or television, or the stage? I think it was a sensible idea to have the preliminary chat with the appointments man, although he doesn't sound to be especially stimulating. Why are they always such sad sacks? Still, I think this is a bridge you don't have to sweat about preparing to cross yet. While it's wise to survey the battlefield in general and to weigh up the best routines for advance, don't expend too much mental energy on the actual campaign yet. Next summer will be soon enough, I think, to start doing anything definite. If you have by then decided that publishing is what you want, we'll get down on paper some specific places to head for. I don't think you'll have any problem about getting in one of the best houses.

The dogs are all right, I suppose, although Duffy and Sally have escaped twice. I think Tris has finally plugged up the dach-size gaps. Very interested to hear your reactions to Dyson. One of the oddities of life is that it is quite possible to like and respect the Other Side! Mother's well and she's at the moment putting in plants and shrubs we bought yesterday. Tris is out shopping and David and Dawn Brend are on their way. Take care of your dear self.

Love and kisses Papa

Annie, referred to in the next letter, was my grandfather's widow. She died of cancer in March 1971. Blanche was my father's cousin.

29 October 1970

Dearest Mandle,

Haven't heard from you for a while; so how is it going back there in the Arctic East? Are you bearing up well against the pressure of the Siberian winds, and of your final year? Do let us know how life's going.

Rather drear news today from Tony Hender: that his mother, Blanche, has been—as we knew she was due to be—taken to hospital and it sounds as if its a recurrence of the cancer for which she was operated on a year or two ago. I don't know if *she* knows precisely what it is, so I should be circumspect; but I shall be talking to Annie next week, anyway. Incidentally, it was brought home to me with a shock by your Mother the other day that its a year since my father died—on November 9. It's quite incredible that the time can have gone so quickly. I imagine Annie may be aware of the nearness of the date, and I'd be very grateful if you could drop her a card. I've written to Fabian, asking him to go and see her; and, should she want to make a journey to the Crematorium, to accompany her. We shall, of course arrange for flowers. I speak to her quite often and she sounds in good form and high spirits, but I gather from Fabe that she tends to lapse a bit into a sort of absentness. Perhaps it's all been rather too much for her, this past year, and the strain has told. But Fabe goes round there and keeps in touch, which is gratifying. She's very fond of him, and I'm sure his visits brighten her day a bit.

It has been a late autumn down here. Until a week ago the leaves hadn't turned all that much and the foliage was still thick; but suddenly the whole countryside has thinned out and become russet. I had a rather dreadful trip up to Edinburgh and back Sunday–Tuesday (it's an appallingly long way, 1,200 miles there and back) and I felt fairly knocked up when I eventually sagged down here. Today was beautiful: strong sun and a viney smell in the air, and I went with Mother into Beaminster where she shopped, and we then turned off toward Netherbury to explore Marshwood Vale, which I'd not been near. We drove below Broadwindsor, through Silkhay (and caught sight of lanky windswept salukis leaping about inside a garden, so doubtless that is Miss W's new joint) and we probed our way down narrow and often blind-end roads, circling South toward Whitchurch Canonicorum, via Shave Cross and Cutty Stubbs and other lost places. It's an extraordinary area; a vast basin of almost empty country rimmed by the hill ranges which link up with Pilsdon Pen. The reason it's empty, I have read, is that the soil here is an impervious clay through which no water rises to supply a settler or through which water doesn't sink in winter, so that it's poor farming country and a bleak, spongy bog in the bad weather.

I had a letter from someone who has a cottage in Powerstock saying that he and his wife often watched a pair of hobbies on E————n and that he thought they bred on the Crutchley's land, which is most exciting.

Have you seen my 'Daily Mail' pieces, by the way? They may interest you as they're mostly about the Mill and surrounds. Did you know that the pigeons are now installed, a cock and 2 hens, very beautiful snowy birds, which seem to be settling in quite happily, tho' God knows how we're going to keep Gally and the dachs from chasing them. They've now taken to hunting moles. There's a mole at large around the swimming pool, so all the lawn there looks like the Somme after heavy bombardment. The dogs have excavated huge craters trying to dig them out, damn them.

We've also arranged for a pair of peafowl to come—this

year's hatching, so they'll be quite small and undecorative for a couple of years.

I think you'll have been seeing Tris today. Do hope the trip went smoothly, for him and that you've had an enjoyable reunion. I don't myself know what the result of his latest round of interviews is, if any, but I do wish he could get the right break. I think he's finding it rather frustrating and a bit depressing now, and it does rather pique me when I know some of the deadbeats who've got inside the BBC. Mother's well and in good spirits.

Do take care of yourself, my dear girl, and put all you've got into this year, because whatever comes after, this will have been invaluable groundwork. I think of you often and wish you well.

Your ever loving Pa

My father was working on a commissioned biography of Harriet Beecher Stowe, which was long overdue and had become a standing joke—and misery—in the family.

In December Tristan at last got a post at BBC Television, Bristol to start in January.

Entrained: between Crewkerne & Sherborne,
8 December 1970

Dearest Poodle,

Am trying to sway with the train but this letter may be indecipherable. It seems so long since I was in direct touch with you altho' I read all your letters home with pleasure and great interest in all your multifarious doings. You sound so spectacularly *busy*—& with so many valuable things, & I don't mean work subjects alone. It's such an exciting period when one has broken into a new field of writing (I'm thinking of you with Faulkner) but anguishing too because the more one reads the more one sees stretching & opening before, behind & sideways: all the author's influences & his contemporaries & the likeminded. The whole Southern school is fascinating & 'regional' in a way unknown in G.B. Among modern Southerners I'd say are worth reading are Eudora Welty, Carson McCullers, Harper Lee, Walker Percy.

It now seems fairly sure that I shall be going off for about a month's filming immediately after Christmas—not to Indonesia but to the South Pacific, probably starting in the Phillipines & on to the New Hebrides, perhaps Tonga (or Samoa) & ending up in Australia (tho' not to film there) ... which should be most interesting although at present I see it as a black, looming threat which puts in jeopardy weekly columns, etc, not to mention the hideous Harriet.

Longing to see you. Are you all equipped for Christmas? I've got Mother's present and her birthday one & am going to try to get F's 21st in London today: gold cufflinks, I think.

Tris arrived home last night. Gathered he very much enjoyed his visit East—altho' he's not very communicative. I wish he weren't so bottled up. He doesn't seem awfully happy (& yet one feels he ought to feel v. positively happy about the job) and it's impossible to know why as he gives no hint beyond a rather poker-faced silence. F. sounds to be happy & well-immersed in work which is super.

It will be so nice to have you all together under one roof. When you come thru' London can you call at the flat—or will that be out of phase with your plans? If you can, shall be most obliged if you can get my spare, repaired leg from the wardrobe & bring it down in the van. It won't be too gruesome: it is in a large bag. I know Mother wants a chair collected from Jean's (which Tris failed to do last week) but this may not be possible for you if you are there at a weekend when the Malberts are likely to be in Langley.

Am going up for a Foyles luncheon at the Dorchester given for the Joan Bakewell/Nicholas Garland book 'The New Priesthood' (all about the TV evil-eye medicine men).

My love as ever
  Papa

The Mill,
16 December

Dearest Mandle,

It seems such an age since I saw you and it is delightful to know that, although for such a short break, you will soon be back here, and that we shall all be gathered together for Christmas. I think our first Christmas at the Mill will be a special occasion.

Tris is busy with Christmassy things before he starts doing a Post Office sorting job on Monday to rake in some cash. He's in much better form.

Now what about news here? Well, the peafowl are installed in the end stable (behind the dogs' kitchen) and they're very lively birds. We're keeping them in for a few more weeks yet, but they're very comfortably accommodated with straw and perches and food and water. I climbed the pigeons' loft to feed them a few days ago, and I noticed that some of the twigs and straw we'd put up there just in case they wanted to line their brooding chambers had been used, and that a nest had been built in one. I felt in and there was an egg! At this time of the year! They're really quite indefatigable. When I went today there was the full clutch of two, so we decided that now it really was quite safe to take off the wire netting at the front of the cote. So this I did this morning. Instantly one of the hens, which was being carnally pursued by the cock, shot out of one of the entrance holes like a blue streak and hasn't been seen since. I terribly fear that she's gone for good. However, the other two shuffled out a bit uncertainly, and then took to wing. It was super to see them in a brilliant blue sunlit sky trying out their wings for the first time. They climbed, and spiralled and circled almost out of sight in the sky, getting their bearings, then eventually came and settled on the roof and spent the rest of the day there and on the barns. I scattered some corn for them on the forecourt and they came down to feed on that, and then returned to the cote for the night. So I think they're safely settled. I'm just hoping that the other will sooner or later home in, but not certain by any means that we shall see it again.

On Friday, after the programme, I went on to the Snows, who were having a party. It was very enjoyable. Mostly painters and gallery directors and people in the art world. Peter and Maria were both delighted to hear that Fabe was at Leeds, which they think very highly of.

I'm still struggling with the appalling Harriet. MUST get it done before Christmas, before I go away. I've got a girl in the village to type the MS for me, so after tomorrow shall try to start feeding her with the opening chapters.

Gally, and Tilly and Duffy are all fine and fairly consistently badly behaved. They have, however, come to a sort of *detente* with the guinea fowl. In this scarcer time I've taken pity on them and taken to scattering corn for them so they spend most of their time on my balcony. But even when they're down on the lawn, the dogs now tend to walk round them and the guinea fowl stay put, so they seem to have grown bored with over-reacting to each other. It's very beautiful here. Do you realise that it's now over a year since Mother and I first saw the Mill? The trees are bare now and there are big flocks of fieldfare in the hedges; lots of holly to cut. There was a vixen barking in the field for a few minutes last night.

Take care of yourself, love. It will be so nice to see you very soon now.

Your affectionate Pa.

At the end of 1970, just after Christmas, my father went off on what turned out to be a two-month BBC film-trip of Australia and the South Pacific Islands. Tristan had begun his job at BBC Bristol.

Goondiwindi,
Queensland,
2 January 1971

Dearest Poo,

I'm sitting in a motel room in this town named Goondiwindi (not a joke from the Barry McKenzie strip) which would remind you of the Mid-West: wide, empty street with soft shoulders and spaced split-level houses and a few gas stations baking under a chromium sun. We're all knackered: we've just (3.30 pm) arrived back from a 260-mile kangeroo hunt in the bush north of here, which started last night at midnight, led by a John Wayne type of 'roo-shooter who holds a rifle in one hand and a spotlight in the other and blasts at the animals from his pickup truck. But (as one expects to be normal on stories) there were no 'roos; so much rain here has covered normally barren plains with grass, and the 'roos disperse and are harder to reach—and are anyway on their way to extermination, which is what our story is about. So we roared down rocky, gulley-riddled dirt roads and thru' creeks in flood all night through (they feed most at night) and by dawn he still hadn't killed one, altho' a few had been sighted. He killed a wild boar, and there was a struggle to knife it in the forest, with his dog hanging onto an ear while it screamed and slashed with its tusks and we were all trying to pull off the dog so that Bill (the Wayne character) could put another .22 slug into it. At 1.30 am I was driving the car with Bill ahead in the pickup truck, and I hit a bog and the car sank up to its axles (we'd already been stranded in a flood and once before in a bog, but managed to be pulled & manhandled out) but this time we were there 3½ hours cutting young trees & stacking them and stones under the wheels and trying to spin it out, while the sun was burning at 90 degrees and one was tortured by flies and mosquitoes, & when we got ours out Bill's truck also sank trying to get through on the pontoon of logs, and we had to start again on that. Eventually we got out & eventually he shot a 'roo and we got a film of him slashing it to bits, and came back to the chiller (the refrig. station) in Goondiwindi from where the meat is sent to factories for pet food.

On Thursday from Sydney I telephoned your Uncle Jack in Melbourne and we talked for about ten minutes. He seems in very good spirits and tremendously looking forward to his visit to England.

I'm much more interested in Australia than I imagined I would be. Its quality is so distinctive and utterly different to anything I've met with before, despite this thin layer of American Suburb feeling about the small towns. The countryside is indescribable: the size and stretch of it, which makes even the United States look built up and local: this isn't mountain country but just unending rolling plains of untouched (or barely touched) scrubby woodland and park-like expanses, full of strange and wonderful birds and beasts. We saw emu grazing; many parrot-like birds which I simply can't identify, and hawks and falcons of unknown kind; the shining air rings with cries which have never before encountered one's ears, and there is a fantastic profusion of butterflies, some sparrow-sized, and even the trees—many of course eucalyptus—are strange to the eye.

I wonder how you all are. Very little news of Britain reaches here. The distance is so great and Australia is totally absorbed in its own hedonistic goings-on of cricket and surfing and local murders, but it's obvious from the snippets we get that the cold continues to grip you. I do hope you're well, love. What did you do on New Year's Eve? We were in the hotel in Sydney and it was a rather damp occasion: the restaurant we ate in closed at 9 pm (as they all do—and that's late!) and we did sit it out upstairs until midnight but there was, apart from a funny hat or two being put on, not much of a celebratory feeling.

I can't predict when I'll next have a chance of actually sitting at a desk for half an hour and writing a letter to any of you—one is always hastening somewhere with bags and notebooks and phone numbers and plane tickets. What a way to earn a living! Although this will be certainly a memorable experience, I'm reminded again that whizzing about the globe isn't for me any more.

I'll try to keep in touch—and try to let the BBC have a forward address for New Guinea and let your Mother know, so you could write if you felt like it.

Take care of yourself.
    All love Pa

Suva Airport
22 January 1971

Darling Poo,

We were up at 4 am theoretically to fly from Fiji to Tonga & (it's now 11.15 am) are slumped in the potting shed-sized 'lounge' while several men hammer desultorily at the DC10 parked on the runway. Fiji seems interesting —what we have seen of it—& v. different from the coral atolls, tufted monotonously with palms, upon which we've been living for the past month. Dramatically jagged mountains, much sugar cane & a more cosmopolitan mixture of Indians (who outnumber Fijians) & every permutation of mixed Polynesian & Mexican blood. Otherwise the Pacific is amazingly like a stage set for 'Sadie Thompson' with a touch of 'Night of the Iguana' —seedy stagnant one-street harbour towns with Shipping Offices, Steamship Stores, & Chinese groceries, Somerset Maugham suburbanites working for copra companies & rather degenerate Conradian beachcombers.

I think the trip is going OK—but gruellingly. We shall have covered 30,000 miles by the time we're back—the distances to be covered on & between stories are immense.

I managed to get a taxi into Suva & found 4 letters from you all, which was super. Thank you so much for all the news & gossip. God knows if you'll get this before I'm home as rumours of a postal strike reach us.

Keep your cool about Finals—I'm *certain* you'll distinguish yourself but even if the luck should be less than good, you will have a Trained Mind.

Had a letter from Tris. So good to know that it's working for him.
 Longing to see you all
 Fondest love, my dear
   Pa

In March, after returning from the South Pacific, Kenneth went to New York, to 'recce' for a film on wildlife in the city.

*The Presidential Special En Route New York,
17 March 1971*

Dearest Poodle,

On this ridiculous Jumbo Jet it is rather like being propelled at 600 mph in a Fortes Hamburger Bar. Nothing works. The mid-Atlantic movie didn't come on the screen & none of the plastic compartments does up. There's headphone 8-way music: The Big Bands; See-mi Classical; Mood Music, etc.

Am ½-way into Michael J. Arlen's biography of his father: *the* light pop, see-mi classical SMART best-seller of the international Cunard Line '20s: 'The Girl in the Green Hat', etc. It's a sad, rootless autobiography, a childhood in Grand Hotels, & governesses & the Corniche (a la Nabokov) & emigré destitute aristocrats, the detritus of the new order '30s. Who was it who said: 'If we live long enough we understand our father—if we're lucky we live long enough to forgive him'? I wonder, not infrequently, if you, & your brothers, will do either. I was immensely affected by your corporate thoughtfulness in sending the flowers, & the message yesterday to your Mother & me. I do value that. It seems to me conceivable at those times that perhaps I haven't been disastrous to you all. I think perhaps none of you fully realise the happiness I gain from you & from seeing you filling out into creative, individual people. I suffer for *you* particularly at this time, having to settle, in hand-to-hand combat, the scholastic score, but you *mustn't* allow these tensions to overcome your innate sense of what is important and relevant—super if you get a splendid degree, but that hasn't been fundamentally why you've been to university. So, whatever else you may find it hard to forgive me for, don't hold *that* against me. Most of all I want you to *express* yourself, & that you have to do in your own style & manner, & *not* according to anyone else's ideas. Be certain of yourself. You have reason to be. You know that you have my love and admiration always. Your Papa

I spent the Easter of 1971 at the Mill in Dorset, revising for finals.
I had begun to worry about what to do when I left university.

The Mill,
17 April 1971

My very dear daughter,

Mainly to double-establish (for you don't need to be told) that you have our warmest, and most confident, wishes for your nearing acid-test. From all I've seen and gathered, you seem to me to have tackled the situation in an exemplary manner, of well-organised work, and that is bound to pay off. I can't say I envy you, but I do admire both the spirit and the system with which you've tackled the job. Now all you need is some good luck in the exams themselves—so here's wishing you vast helpings of it!

I've been reflecting a little on your future activities after all this is over. I understand from Mother that you're still far from being seized by a vocational fervency for anything in particular, and that she floated the thought of doing a year's VSO. I'm bound to say that I couldn't support that idea. Of course, I'm not for a second trying to tell you what you should do, but it may be of help if I tell you the way I see your situation. I feel that your leanings toward an academic career will be worth pursuing only if you get a brilliant degree, which would propel you into some of the more desirable and elitist areas. This is being quite calculatedly hard-eyed about it. Below that level the educational second-best can be pretty drab and stodgy as a life: I mean 30 years in Aberystwyth or something similar. Still, there are of course other ways of seeing this—branching out abroad, etc. In any event, I don't think spending yet another year doing what might well in itself be fascinating but which is likely to be a period of treading water before pushing off and swimming is at this point going to serve you best. I think you'd be well advised to charge pellmell into a field before you feel too old to start at a point equal to that of others two or three years younger than you. I also understand from Mother that you're thinking of writing to the BBC. I would strongly support this. Although I am convinced that you could succeed conspicuously in journalism, I am equally convinced you could do well on either side of the camera. You know I wouldn't dissemble about this. If I felt that you'd be no good at it, I would say so, for it would be an unkindness as well as idle to encourage you into something where you would be both unhappy and incapable. On the contrary. I know that you would be a most valuable asset to any programme. Now the snags. You know the difficulty Tris had. The period of expansion in the BBC, and I suppose on the other side, has slowed down, and there were about three Oxbridge graduates taken out of 5,000 applications last year. I would certainly make a head-on application. It might mean starting in any capacity you can tunnel in at. I am absolutely confident that once you were in such an organisation you could quite quickly get through to the creative and responsible kind of post you could so well handle. You must have no false modesty about this, or sense of inadequacy. Let me assure you, quite factually and detachedly (without any parental fondness hazing my eyes) that, although on a programme like '24 Hours' there are a few exceptionally outstanding and brilliant minds, the majority of the production staff who sluggishly flow through that office have no right to be there at all: I don't know how on earth many of them managed to penetrate what ought to be quite exacting standards of professionalism. I don't mean this as a back-handed compliment when I say that you couldn't be less qualified than many. No more lecturing. But do let me know if you want me to canvass around at the BBC and see what possibilities there may be.

It's a beautiful afternoon here after days of blanketing sea-mist. The greater-spotted woodpecker was on the birdtable again; the buzzard wheeled over yesterday (it's rather fabulous having a buzzard over one's garden, isn't it?); 38 species of bird in and around the garden so far. Mother and I were pretty desolate and anxious last night—Tilly and Duffy disappeared for hours on end, and Mother was convinced they were drowned. Long after dark, we were probing around in the fields with torches. They reappeared out of the darkness about 10 pm, caked with soil, and had obviously been rabbiting down deep warrens. Don't bother writing, love, except to say if you want any books sent, or want me to make any enquiries.

Every good wish and my fondest love Pa

*The Mill,
8 May 1971*

Darling Mandle,

It was so nice hearing your voice on the line today, & to judge from it you are totally in control of your destiny and fate, with the lightest hand on the tiller. Truly, loved one, we do understand the sense you must have of being in the maximum impact point of a disaster area & strategic target, with the sirens wailing louder every second, but 'Twill soon be a memory and will scale down to its correct perspective in your life. In the meantime try to strike the delicate balance of not being overcome while at the same time taking it seriously enough to be master of the situation. We shall be sweating with you, anyway, and hoping for good luck in the papers you get and that the wind is blowing in the right direction and spring flowers are in blossom and the balance of payments is in good shape and the German mark holding its own and ping-pong games in progress between East and West all other signs and omens are propitious.

A gorgeous day here today, although there was an unseasonal keenness in the air despite the sunshine. Gally, as you know, has had her gynaecological op, poor thing, and your Mother brought her back in a whoozy, drunken state, with her legs buckling under her and swathed in bandages. She was really marvellously good. Today she had her stitches out, and is very much better, but she is feeling very sorry for herself, and slumps in a corner gazing accusingly at us with bloodshot eyes, and demonstrating why the term hangdog was invented. I think now she's really rather enjoying being fussed over and everyone making sympathetic and consoling noises, and she's rather acting up to it, like Elizabeth Barratt Browning.

I had an outing on to Eggardon last week with Brian Jackman, the young man on the Sunday Times who has a cottage at Powerstock. He showed me the way over the high bluff, and we walked along a ridge which reminded me of Baggy Point, do you remember? It's an immense limestone promontory, with the land scooping away in immensity to rough woodland and vales where deer and foxes wander. Meadow pipits were singing, and linnets, and kestrels hanging over the hillsides, and we watched a buzzard spiralling out of the distant oak forest of Powerstock Common & up on a thermal. And while up there we saw a VERY RARE BIRD, [The Montague's Harrier, which nested and bred for one season] which I will tell you about, but which must be treated with fantastic circumspection.

The dam isn't working properly; Duffy and Tilly escaped again; I can't get proper work done on either my New York script or my book, and fritter away the days in the midst of what Rene Cutforth in this week's Listener calls 'writer's blight'. Don't take up writing; take up something harmonious and flowing and tangible which doesn't mean scraping your breastbone bare all the time, like cooking scones for a little bow-windowed shop in Beaminster.

Take care, my dear, and put your trust in God and a benign, well-fed and happily-married external examiner.

(Your affectionate Papa)

I graduated in June 1971. I spent a few weeks in Israel, then returned to London to start seriously looking for work. My father had assumed for some time that I would go into journalism—an assumption I happily went along with.

He was in the process of moving from his small flat in St John's Wood to one in Notting Hill.

The Mill,
6 October 1971

Dearest Mandle,

Delighted to hear you've fixed on a flat, which will remove one of the pressing problems and release your thought and energy for the Job!

I imagine you must be a bit hard up. Here's a bit to keep you going.

As you suggested, it would be nice—and perhaps a useful time now—to meet next week. Could you have lunch with me on Monday—the 11th? I shall be more available than I usually am on a Monday (I hope) as I won't be travelling up that morning. I have to do a day's recording at Southampton on Sunday, so shall travel up to London on Sunday evening and spend the night in the wreckage and debris of the flat, so shall be at Lime Grove promptly Monday am. If you could manage to get along there about noon, or really any time around lunch-time, we could go down to the club.

I think it would be extremely valuable if we could have a general talk about your programme now that you've got living place settled. Try not to get too dispirited and disheartened; it's a bad time, but anyway it's never, except by the utmost luck, easy to bore in at the right place. I think its a very sensible move to take up this typing improvement course—but we have to make sure that you don't get stuck in a typing job. I'll bring up your curriculum vitae and when you've approved it I can get it run off and xeroxed so you'll have plenty of copies to spare.

Also we must have a preliminary talk about the structure of the poetry reading. I think we ought to script it out a bit.

Do hope to be seeing you on Monday.

Yr ever loving Pa

My father spent a couple of weeks in South America on a BBC film trip in January 1972.

Flying between Caracas & Antigua,
19 January 1972

Darling Mandle,

Back after an Action-Packed 10 days which really was a fascinating experience—scarlet ibis in the mangrove swamps of the lagoons of Eastern Venezuala, Caymans (alligators) in the roadside swamps, hummingbirds in the hotel 'tropical gardens' inside the drinking (drunken) area; also marvellous in your actual steaming jungle around Canaima with ocelot, jaguar, tapir, etc.

How are you, my dear? I hope you are happy and sanguine. I think you've had a v. testing time since graduating & admire the way you have stuck it out and gone on chipping away at what attracts you: it's the only way, but it is not an easy way, yet you have not been deterred and that is the best stand to take in the long run.

What makes me particularly happy is that the three of you stay in such close and trusting contact. The Allsops (by observable family history) tend to be a fractious lot & their blood seems often to be thinner than water—so it is so good to see you & your brothers so loyal and loving towards each other. This is something I've been wanting to say for some time but somehow the exigencies of living seem to operate against its expression: so aircraft & the limbo they impose do, oddly enough, give one the fleeting interlude in which to say these neglected things. Don't let it lapse in later life. Perhaps, as an only child, I put undue weight on the value of family & having those you can rely upon & come to—but I don't really think so. I think you three *have* got an exceptionally sound relationship, and it matters to me very deeply that it lasts for you all.

How nice it will be to be out of that Latin-American garbage-heap, where all the 3 million inhabitants of Caracas have 3 million beat-up Pontiacs spreading a blanket of smog.

Take care of your dear self,
All my love Pa

It wasn't until I'd spent several months battling with every available weapon to get into journalism that I realised that I wasn't really prepared to push hard enough or to take very much of the graft, and that therefore I wasn't committed enough to journalism. I turned all my forces towards publishing, which appealed much more, and after another period of battling and further unemployment, I was offered a job in educational publishing, beginning in February 1972.

My father accepted the change happily once he realised I was serious.

While I was in London, we met up frequently for a meal or a drink.

Since leaving university I had been making notes with a view to a novel. During 1972 my ideas began to crystallise and the novel became an increasingly important part of my life.

I decided, also, to live on my own, and moved into a single flat in Notting Hill.

The Mill,
27 July 1972

Dearest Poodle,

What a nice relaxed and happy evening that was together: how silly it is that we so seldom find time for those kind of meetings. It was good to be able to talk to you so fully about your activities. I really do think that having got settled in your own roost will give you the cornerstone you needed.

Riding down on the train, I was reading the current issue of the 'New York Review of Books', on three novels reviewed by Thomas R. Edwards. None of the novels sounded especially good—by Michael Crichton, who wrote 'The Andromeda Strain', by Frederik Bucchner, a hackish story-teller, I think, and by Isaac Bashevis Singer, more 'Rich Jewish Fables'—but Edwards has some perceptive things to say about the novel which struck me as a continuation of some of the problems of writing about, or out of, one's experience. He says that most novels really have to be considered as commodities, produced and distributed like frozen peas, and goes on: '. . . since a world full of people doesn't usually feel like a world full of God, the novel from its beginnings has dwelt upon the secular life, men and women making do in a realm God hasn't visited for quite a while. Here people are on their own, they have careers instead of vocations, stories don't always predict their own endings, meaning is not found in events but gets attached to them more or less provisionally.' (Very much the difficulty John Fowles was trying to overcome in 'The French Lt's Woman': deliberately leaving options open and resisting being held, as the writer, to the predetermined line which his mind had tried to impose upon him.) Edwards continues: 'Living in a world whose mysteries may be meaningless, secular man is necessarily man in trouble. Rather than learning truth, he can at best only solve problems, and his temporal rewards, like money and marriage, seem finally enigmatic or ambiguous, spiritually speaking. The novelist may heroically settle for social blessings, as Jane Austen and Fielding did, or like Dickens, James and Tolstoy, he may weigh the compromising costs of social accomplishment, how it shall not profit a man to gain the world. But genuine mystery always comes out as something of an embarrassment.' His criticism of the Crichton style of writing—I mean kind of writing—is a sounding alarm: this book he says, 'accepts the inertness of fact. Once something has happened, right there on the page, there's nothing to do but have something else happen . . . [his novel] records events whose meaning and consequences are unalterable.'

I don't think you should worry too much about your 'plot' because there aren't such things in life, therefore nor in convincing novels about life. Of course, actions and events have consequences (sometimes, not always) and it can be amusing and/or frightening to see how they resurface in their random way at a later stage—but they are so often self-deciding. . . . Just an attempt to define, better, a point I was touching upon.

I've just remembered that you'll be here tomorrow, so I shan't post this but leave it here for you.

    Your ever loving Papa

Notting Hill,
16 November 1972

Dear father,

I won't be around tomorrow after all—The Conformist is on at the Electric, and Tuesday is the only night that both Gordon and I can go (and we have planned to go together).

I have been trying to check up on the architecture of the Anglo-Saxons. My curiosity has been aroused—I can't believe that local farmers would have destroyed completely Athelstan's castle, while leaving good solid relics of King John. So: it emerges that while you're correct about stone, it wasn't the commonest building material. Pre-Norman buildings would have been constructed of wood, stone, brick or a mixture of either two or three of these...' so the castle no doubt did comprise of degradable material as well as stone.

My source isn't all that good. I'd like to learn a lot more. It's fascinating to discover the strength of the Saxon culture—for remnants (of building, clothes, pottery, literature, music, etc) to still be with us and influencing us—despite the Norman influx—is amazing. I can't see much of our present culture surviving—and there's not much I'd want to see around in 1,000 years time.

Anyway, there you are.

I probably won't see you this week, but do call next week. I would enjoy a meal with you. If you just let me know that you'll be around on a particular evening, I'll wait.

Much love Mandy

*Notting Hill,
1 am, 18 November 1972*

Darling Mandle,

I am sorry not to have answered your note straight away but today was pellmell & last evening (after my takeaway Kentucky Fried Chicken & Jamaica date astie, served by a Pak in Portobello Rd's China Town) I had to work on 'Edition' scripts. Now, I have just got back from doing it: I think a punchy show but at the cost of terminal exhaustion.

That's interesting stuff on the Anglo-Saxon Freddie Mintons you dug up. You must have a look through my Dorset library: quite extensive now. I dare say there'll be some quite specific stuff to be found there. Hope you enjoyed the flicks—& the theatre tomorrow.

All love Pa

My work in educational publishing gave me an interest in education. I applied for, and was offered, a place at Exeter University Department of Education for October 1973. I took the opportunity to leave my job early in the year and give myself a sabbatical. My writing hadn't been going well, so I decided at Christmas to take the time off before going to Exeter to finish my novel.

The Mill,
6 January 1973

Dearest Mandle,

I have been unhappy about the zigzag of lightning dissonance in what was otherwise such a nice evening & I am sorry for my disproportionately cutting words (I was in a pretty exhausted state, therefore, I'm afraid, a bit over-strung & nerves easily snapped). Although we Made Up, I don't think that in the conversation that followed I sufficiently well put my attitude to your plan to try to prove that you can be the writer you want to be. In other words, I want you to know that I'm not merely willing to give any help I can, but that (a) I admire your spirit & determination to do this & (b) have a certainty in my bones that you have it in you—one develops an instinct for picking out the real writer from the would-be writer & I *know* you're in the first tiny minority.

But don't let this loom too large as a traumatic test for yourself. Certainly put your back into it, but be relaxed about it & *enjoy the period*: serious but not do-or-die! Just work concentratedly but unflurried—& don't feel that you have got to produce something of shattering significance out of it.

You have grown into such a worthwhile person—you give me much inner joy (not often enough vocalised). I want you to be happy about this sabbatical—write not as if a sword is suspended over your head but like a bird on the wing.

Fondest love, as ever, Papa

That was the last letter he wrote to me.

I left my job in April and moved into a small cottage in the grounds of the Mill, in Dorset, and began to write.

On 11 May my parents went to Exeter for the West Country Writers' Congress, where my father met up with a very dear, and briefly estranged, friend, Henry Williamson. 'There were warm greetings all round', my father wrote in his diary.

He had recently been fitted with a new artificial leg, which caused him pain and despondency.

But there were compensations. The weekend of 18–21 May, my parents went to Wales, and were exhilarated by the countryside and the birdlife. 20 May was a 'red letter day'—two kites, two buzzards, a kestrel, and a peregrine falcon and tiercel sighted in one spot.

On the way back to Dorset on 21 May he returned to watch the peregrines and 'felt satisfied and full of delight for them'.

On 23 May, he died.